HOMO-SEXUALITY & GAY RIGHTS

IDEAS in CONFLICT

Gary E. McCuen

publications inc.

411 Mallalieu Drive
Hudson, Wisconsin 54016
Phone (715) 386-7113

Illustrations & Photo Credits

Carol & Simpson 11, Mark Cullum 93, Gary Markstein 141, Henry Paine 133, 146, Steve Sack 87, Bill Sanders 31, Sargent 127, Jeff Stahler 73, Toles 77, Dan Wasserman 151, Richard Wright 82.

publications inc.

© 1994 by Gary E. McCuen Publications, Inc.
411 Mallalieu Drive, Hudson, Wisconsin 54016

(715) 386-7113

International Standard Book Number
ISBN 0-86596-094-1
Printed in the United States of America

CONTENTS

CHAPTER 3 **HOMOSEXUALS AND THE MILITARY**

CHAPTER 4 **THE GAY FAMILY**

CHAPTER 5 THE GAY RIGHTS MOVEMENT

REASONING SKILL DEVELOPMENT

These activities may be used as individualized study guides for students in libraries and resource centers or as discussion catalysts in small group and classroom discussions.

IDEAS in CONFLICT ®

This series features ideas in conflict on political, social, and moral issues. It presents counterpoints, debates, opinions, commentary, and analysis for use in libraries and classrooms. Each title in the series uses one or more of the following basic elements:

Introductions that present an issue overview giving historic background and/or a description of the controversy.

Counterpoints and debates carefully chosen from publications, books, and position papers on the political right and left to help librarians and teachers respond to requests that treatment of public issues be fair and balanced.

Symposiums and forums that go beyond debates that can polarize and oversimplify. These present commentary from across the political spectrum that reflect how complex issues attract many shades of opinion.

A **global** emphasis with foreign perspectives and surveys on various moral questions and political issues that will help readers to place subject matter in a less culture-bound and ethnocentric frame of reference. In an ever-shrinking and interdependent world, understanding and cooperation are essential. Many issues are global in nature and can be effectively dealt with only by common efforts and international understanding.

Reasoning skill study guides and discussion activities provide ready-made tools for helping with critical reading and evaluation of content. The guides and activities deal with one or more of the following:

RECOGNIZING AUTHOR'S POINT OF VIEW

INTERPRETING EDITORIAL CARTOONS

VALUES IN CONFLICT

WHAT IS EDITORIAL BIAS?

WHAT IS SEX BIAS?

WHAT IS POLITICAL BIAS?

WHAT IS ETHNOCENTRIC BIAS?

WHAT IS RACE BIAS?

WHAT IS RELIGIOUS BIAS?

*From across **the political spectrum** varied sources are presented for research projects and classroom discussions. Diverse opinions in the series come from magazines, newspapers, syndicated columnists, books, political speeches, foreign nations, and position papers by corporations and nonprofit institutions.*

About the Editor

Gary E. McCuen is an editor and publisher of anthologies for public libraries and curriculum materials for schools. Over the past years his publications have specialized in social, moral and political conflict. They include books, pamphlets, cassettes, tabloids, filmstrips and simulation games, many of them designed from his curriculums during 11 years of teaching junior and senior high school social studies. At present he is the editor and publisher of the *Ideas in Conflict* series and the *Editorial Forum* series.

CHAPTER 1

HOMOSEXUALITY AND BIOLOGY

HOMOSEXUALITY AND BIOLOGY

STUDY SUGGESTS BIOLOGICAL ASPECT TO HOMOSEXUALITY

Washington Post

The following article appeared in the Washington Post. *It describes a study on brain tissue that suggests a biological aspect to homosexuality.*

Points to Consider:

1. Summarize research findings on the relevance of hypothalamus node size to homosexuality.

2. Until 1973, what had been the prevailing concept of homosexuality?

3. What does research report concerning environmental factors and homosexuality?

4. What evidence shows a genetic influence on homosexuality?

"We know that being gay runs in families," said Pillard, the Boston University psychiatrist, who has conducted studies of the phenomenon.

Are homosexuals born gay and heterosexuals born straight, or is sexual orientation shaped by some combination of upbringing, choice and environment?

Debate on these questions, the source of controversy in science and society for centuries, is about to be sparked anew because evidence has been found that homosexuality may have a biological component.

Neuroscientist Simon LeVay of the Salk Institute in San Diego reports in *Science* that, in at least one critical region, the brain structures of gay and straight men appear to be dramatically different.

HYPOTHALAMUS

The area LeVay examined, part of a deep interior formation called the hypothalamus, is known to be involved in regulating sexual behavior. One tiny node of that organ, LeVay's tissue studies found, is nearly three times larger in heterosexual males than in homosexual males.

His research also disclosed that the anatomical form of that node — which is about as big as a grain of sand and contains only a few thousand nerve cells — is remarkably similar in women and gay males, and that the form is substantially different in heterosexual males.

"If this research holds up, it would be the first physiological difference of this kind ever shown," said psychiatrist Richard C. Pillard of Boston University School of Medicine.

Dr. Thomas R. Insel, a behavioral neuroscientist at the National Institute of Mental Health in Rockville, Md., said, "It's quite a striking observation, and as far as I know it's unprecedented. Simon LeVay is a top-notch, world-class neuroanatomist, and this is a very provocative paper."

It is unclear whether the size of the node might have an active role in determining sexual orientation. LeVay emphasized that it could also be an effect of sexual orientation or simply a nonsexual anatomical feature that happens to be correlated with homosexuality. But based on current understanding of brain development, he

"We don't discriminate against homosexuals in this company. As a matter of fact, we've already set up an office for you."

Cartoon by Carol & Simpson. Reprinted with permission.

concluded, it "seems more likely" that the size of the critical cell area "is established early in life and later influences sexual behavior."

SEXUAL BEHAVIOR

Neuroscientists long have known that certain cell clusters called interstitial nuclei on the front of the hypothalamus control sexual behavior and that those structures are much larger in men than in women. Experiments have shown that when those nodes are damaged in male monkeys, heterosexual behavior is impaired but sexual drive remains intact.

So LeVay set out to investigate whether the node would be large in "individuals sexually oriented toward women" and small in those attracted to men, no matter what their sex. He obtained brain tissue from routine autopsies of 41 persons who died at several hospitals in New York and California.

Nineteen were homosexual men who died of complications of AIDS, 16 were "presumed" heterosexual men (of whom six were intravenous drug users who also died of AIDS) and six were heterosexual women, one of whom died of AIDS.

Ironically, the conditions that made LeVay's findings possible could cast doubt on his results. Because sexual orientation is not usually noted on death records, "brain tissue from individuals known to be homosexual has only become available as a result of the AIDS epidemic," he said; and because the disease can affect the brain, "I was worried that the difference might be caused by AIDS."

That is unlikely, he concluded, because the size difference was pronounced between heterosexuals who had AIDS and homosexuals who had AIDS. Nonetheless, LeVay said, to confirm his findings, "we need tissue from gay men who died of other causes."

LeVay's work — which follows a report from the Netherlands last year showing apparent gay-straight differences in another, non-sex-related part of the brain — is expected to reinforce the position of those who believe that sexual orientation is largely determined by heredity rather than social or environmental factors.

That is also the emerging consensus policy of the American Psychiatric Association (APA). "We do tend to feel that there probably is some kind of genetic link," said Richard Isay, a psychiatrist at Cornell Medical College and chairman of the APA's committee on gay, lesbian and bisexual issues.

A DISEASE

As recently as 20 years ago, that was a heretical notion. Until then the medical establishment had generally regarded homosexuality as a disease. Such views, which arose as early as the late 18th century, persisted until 1973, when the APA removed homosexuality from its official roster of mental illnesses.

For most of the 20th century, the prevailing concept (still embraced today by orthodox Freudians and some other psychoanalysts) has been that male homosexuality originates in failure of the child to separate himself from feelings of "unity" with the mother in early infancy and to begin to identify with the father.

Some theorized that this situation was caused by malfunctions in the "Oedipus complex", a phase in which a boy is presumed to compete with his father for the affections of his mother. Others stressed the role of withdrawn fathers or neurotically possessive, "binding" mothers in preventing development of the son's independent male identity.

12

GENETIC LINK

Scientists have uncovered new evidence that genetic factors may play an important — if not dominant — role in determining whether males become homosexual.

In a study of 167 gay men and their brothers conducted at Northwestern and Tufts Universities, researchers found that the genes men inherit from their parents may account for as much as 70 percent of the probability that a male will become gay.

"Male Homosexuality May Have Strong Genetic Link," **Washington Post**, September, 1992

NEW RESEARCH

In recent years, however, that classic psychoanalytic view has been challenged by two forms of research. The first, based on extensive clinical studies of male homosexuals, indicates that there is little, if any, discernible difference between gays and straights in terms of family backgrounds and parental dynamics.

"There seem to be just as many binding mothers and absent or aloof fathers among heterosexuals as among homosexuals," Isay said. "In general, we believe now that environmental factors do not play a significant role in the origins of homosexuality, although they may have an influence on the way sexual orientation is expressed."

A second line of research has turned up considerable evidence for a genetic influence on homosexuality.

"We know that being gay runs in families," said Pillard, the Boston University psychiatrist who has conducted studies of the phenomenon. Gay males, he said, appear to be about four to five times more likely to have bisexual or homosexual brothers than do heterosexuals (22 percent compared to 4 percent). Studies of identical twins usually confirm those patterns. But because there are rare instances in which identical twins adopt different sexual orientations, Pillard said, "we conclude that there must be some environmental factor playing a role."

LeVay's discovery, said neurologist Dennis Landis of Case Western Reserve University in Cleveland, "would begin to suggest why male homosexuality is present in most human populations, despite cultural constraints. It suggests it's a biological phenomenon."

13

2   HOMOSEXUALITY AND BIOLOGY

FLAWED SCIENCE NURTURES GENETIC ORIGIN

Robert Knight

Robert Knight is the Director of Cultural Studies at the Family Research Council in Washington, D.C. The following article appeared in the newsletter In Focus, *a publication of the Council.*

Points to Consider:

1. How does Knight compare alcoholism to homosexuality?

2. Why does Knight call Americans a "therapeutic society" in our attitude toward homosexuality?

3. Comment: "Variations (in the hypothalamus) may be the result, not the cause, of sexual activity."

4. What are the political ramifications of homosexuality being viewed as a genetic condition?

Robert Knight, "Flawed Science Nurtures Genetic Origin for Homosexuality," **In Focus**, 1993. Reprinted with permission of Robert H. Knight, Director of Cultural Studies, Family Research Council in Washington.

The idea that homosexuals are born, not made, is compelling because it appeals to Americans' sense of fairness and tolerance.

Several recent studies indicate that homosexuality may be an inborn trait. This idea is crucial to the homosexual rights movement, which compares sexual orientation to immutable characteristics like race. If a person cannot control sexual preference any more than skin color, why not extend special civil rights protections to homosexuals?

PROBLEMS

There are two problems with this. First, there is no reliable scientific evidence that homosexuality has a genetic basis. Second, even if there were, this would not be reason to condone or promote homosexual behavior. Alcoholics may have a genetically-derived predisposition toward alcohol abuse, but we do not urge them to give in to this impulse just because "that's the way they are." Society also discourages adultery, even if some people with overcharged sexual appetites are severely tempted. Similarly, homosexual behavior is what marks a person as a homosexual, not inclination, which can be temporary, controlled or even changed, as evidenced by the existence of thousands of former homosexuals.

The idea that homosexuals are born, not made, is compelling because it appeals to Americans' sense of fairness and tolerance. It also fits our therapeutic society's increasing desire to avoid individual responsibility for behaviorial choices. But the fact remains that studies cited to "prove" that homosexuality is genetic are flawed and are not replicated.

In the March, 1993 edition of the *Archives of General Psychiatry* (AGP), Drs. William Byne and Bruce Parsons examine past and current claims and conclude that "there is no evidence at present to substantiate a biologic theory . . . the appeal of current biologic explanations for sexual orientation may derive more from dissatisfaction with the present status of psychosocial explanations than from a substantiating body of experimental data."[1]

GAY TWINS

Ironically, this important review is in the very same AGP edition that includes a highly publicized study about lesbian twins. Conducted by J. Michael Bailey and Richard C. Pillard, two

15

researchers who made news in 1991 with a male twins study with similar results,[2] the lesbian study[3] concludes that about half of the lesbians in the sample with identical twins had a twin who was lesbian. Thus, the authors surmise that lesbianism may have at least a partly genetic origin.

Both studies by Bailey and Pillard are flawed. The twins were recruited through advertisements in partisan homosexual publications, which presumably are read mainly by those who identify with the aims of the homosexual rights movement. Also, the twins were raised in the same household. Research strongly indicates that environmental factors play a crucial part in gender-identity formation. (See, for instance the review of environmental studies in Dr. Joseph Nicolosi's *Reparative Therapy of Male Homosexuality*, Jason Aronson, Inc., Northvale, N.J., 1991.)

The Bailey-Pillard studies' non-twin siblings showed a frequency rate for homosexual siblings similar to that of adoptive siblings with no shared genetic inheritance whatever. Also, nowhere are the unique psychological dynamics of twins taken into account, nor other factors such as age at the earliest sexual experiences, or whether one or both of the twins was ever sexually molested. Finally, the fact that nearly half of the homosexual twins' identical siblings were heterosexual should dampen the idea that homosexuality is genetically-based. If it were genetic, then 100 percent of the twins would be homosexual.

SIMON LEVAY

Another highly publicized 1991 study is by former Salk Institute researcher Simon LeVay, who studied a cluster of neurons known as INAH3 (the third interstitial hypothalamus) in the brains of 35 male cadavers.[4] Contrasting 19 known homosexuals with 16 supposedly

16

heterosexual men, LeVay found that the homosexuals generally had smaller clusters. Problems include an extremely small sample size and failure to identify one of the control groups. LeVay didn't know the orientation of the "heterosexual" cadavers, and assumed they were all heterosexual, even though six had died of AIDS. The study also included major exceptions. Three of the "heterosexuals" had clusters smaller than the mean size for the homosexuals. Three of the homosexuals had larger clusters than the mean size for "heterosexuals". Furthermore, it is unclear what role the nodes play, if any, in sexual orientation. Variations may be the result, not the cause, of sexual activity, or of AIDS-related brain damage. Allen and Gorski's 1992 study[5] shows a pattern of different sizes of the brain's anterior commissure between a group of heterosexual men and a group of women and homosexual men. But as Byne and Parsons point out, this study has "many of the same interpretive difficulties as LeVay's..." These include a "tremendous" number of exceptions, such as that 27 of 30 homosexual men had anterior commissures that "fell within the range established by 30 heterosexual men."

POPULAR JOURNALS

Flawed or misreported science can have enormous political ramifications, as shown by the willingness of popular journals to tout studies that bolster gay activists' views while ignoring others that contradict them. The now-discredited Kinsey-based myth[6] that 10 percent of the population is homosexual is a prime example. Although numerous studies from many nations indicate that the percentage is 2% or less,[7] the 10% myth lives on. Even a character in the comic strip "For Better or Worse" proclaimed recently in 1,700 newspapers that homosexual teens are "one in ten!!"

Someday, scientists may find a hereditary condition that makes some people particularly susceptible to the environmental factors that may tend to produce a homosexual orientation. But this is a far cry from finding a "gay gene". It may take years to undo the misconceptions created by a handful of misinterpreted studies.

"The least deviation from the truth is later multiplied a thousand times," Aristotle said. And more recently, Bob Dylan observed that the truth, which eventually wins out, is "a slow train coming".

ENDNOTES

[1]William Byne and Bruce Parsons, "Human Sexual Orientation: The Biologic Theories Reappraised," **Archives of General Psychiatry**, Vol. 50, March 1993, pp. 228-239.

[2]J. Michael Bailey, Richard C. Pillard, "A Genetic Study of Male Sexual Orientation," **Archives of General Psychiatry**, Vol. 48, 1991, pp. 1089-1096.

[3]J. Michael Bailey, Richard C. Pillard, Michael C. Neale, Yvonne Agyei, "Heritable Factors Influence Sexual Orientation in Women," **Archives of General Psychiatry**, Vol. 50, March 1993, pp. 217-223.

[4]Simon LeVay, "A Difference in Hypothalamic Structure Between Heterosexual and Homosexual Men," **Science**, Vol. 258, 1991, pp. 1034-1037.

[5]L.S. Allen, R.A. Gorski, "Sexual Orientation and the Size of the Anterior Commissure in the Human Brain," **Proc Natl Acad Sci U S A**. 1992, Vol. 89, pp. 7199-7202, cited in Byne and Parsons, op. cit., p. 235.

[6]See Judith A. Reisman and Edward W. Eichel, **Kinsey, Sex and Fraud: The Indoctrination of a People,** J. Gordon Muir and John H. Court, editors, Huntington House, Lafayette, LA, 1990.

[7]J. Gordon Muir, "Homosexuals and the 10% Fallacy," **The Wall Street Journal**, March 31, 1993, p. A-14.

3   HOMOSEXUALITY AND BIOLOGY

MAJOR GENETIC COMPONENT FOR HOMOSEXUALITY

Robert Pool

Robert Pool wrote the following article for Science. *It describes a study by Dean Hamer of the National Cancer Institute. This study found evidence for a homosexuality gene.*

Points to Consider:

1. What was the finding of the Hamer study?

2. What led Hamer's group to focus on the X chromosome?

3. How difficult is it to locate a specific gene, given the Xq28 region?

4. According to Hamer, does homosexuality rise solely from genetics?

Robert Pool, "Evidence for Homosexuality," **Science**, Vol. 261, July 16, 1993.

Researchers familiar with the work say this study appears to have a very good chance of holding up.

How much of sexual orientation is determined by a person's genes, and how much by familial and cultural influences? That has proved to be an exceptionally controversial question. Several recent studies of twins and adoptive siblings have pointed toward a large genetic component in homosexuality, implying that a gene or genes should exist that create a predisposition for homosexuality, but there was no direct proof. Now, a team of geneticists at the National Cancer Institute has come closer to that proof.

Dean Hamer and his colleagues Stella Hu, Victoria Magnuson, Nan Hu, and Angela Pattatucci report linking some instances of male homosexuality to a small stretch of DNA on the X chromosome. If the finding can be confirmed, it might eventually lead to a better understanding of the biological basis of homosexuality and of sexual orientation in general.

No one is breaking out the champagne just yet, however. The field of behavioral genetics is littered with apparent discoveries that were later called into question or retracted. Over the past few years, several groups of researchers have reported locating genes for various mental illnesses — manic depression, schizophrenia, alcoholism — only to see their evidence evaporate after they assembled more evidence or reanalyzed the original data. "There's almost no finding that would be convincing by itself in this field," notes Elliot Gershon, chief of the clinical neurogenetics branch of the National Institute of Mental Health. "We really have to see an independent replication."

Despite the caution, researchers familiar with Hamer's work say this study appears to have a very good chance of holding up because it avoids some of the methodological problems of earlier work. One way or the other, the verdict may be in before the end of the year since a replication can probably be performed quickly.

GAY GENE

To look for a possible homosexuality gene, Hamer and his colleagues took a two-step approach. First they recruited 76 homosexual men and traced out pedigrees for each, determining which other members of each family were themselves homosexual. They found 13.5% of the gay men's brothers to be homosexual — much higher than the rate of 2% or so that the Hamer group measured in the gen-

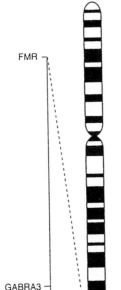

FMR

GABRA3

DX552

G6PD
F8C

DXS1108

DXY5154

q28

eral population. (While this is lower than previous estimates of 4% to 10%, other recent studies have come up with similar low figures.) Earlier studies had also found that brothers of homosexual men are more likely to be homosexual than are men in the general population.

But once Hamer and colleagues ventured outside the immediate family, they found something new. "When we collected the family histories," Hamer says, "we saw more gay relatives on the maternal side than on the paternal side." In particular they found homosexuality to be significantly more common among maternal uncles of gay men and among cousins who were sons of maternal aunts than it is among males in the general population.

This implied that, for some male homosexuals at least, the trait is passed through female members of the family. And this in turn gave the researchers an obvious place to start looking for a homosexuality gene: the X chromosome, the only chromosome inherited exclusively from the mother.

To search for such a gene, Hamer recruited 40 pairs of homosexual brothers, took DNA samples from each, and performed a genetic linkage analysis using gene markers. The idea behind the analysis is simple: on average, each pair of brothers will have about half the DNA on their X chromosomes (and other chromosomes) in common. If both brothers are homosexual because they inherited a particular gene on the X chromosome, the gene must lie somewhere in the shared sections of the chromosome, which can be identified by the gene markers. The researcher examines many pairs of brothers, looking for a stretch of DNA that all or most of them have in common. If such a stretch exists, then it probably contains the target gene.

When Hamer and colleagues performed their analysis, they found that such a shared stretch did indeed exist. Of the 40 pairs of brothers, 33 pairs shared a set of five markers located near the end of the long arm of the X chromosome in a region designated Xq28. It's unlikely the linkage between the markers and the homosexuality trait was due to chance, Hamer says. The linkage has a LOD score of 4.0 — a technical measure that translates to a 99.5% certainty that there is a gene (or genes) in this area of the X chromosome that predisposes a male to become homosexual.

MALE HOMOSEXUALITY

Hamer warns, however, that this one site cannot explain all male homosexuality. Although his pedigree analysis showed that the homosexuality trait is usually maternally inherited, he did see some families where the trait seemed to be passed on paternally. And even among his 40 sets of brothers, chosen so that there was no evidence of the trait passing through male family members, seven sets of brothers did not share the stretch of Xq28 where the gene appears to lie. Instead, Hamer says, it seems likely that homosexuality arises from a variety of causes, genetic and perhaps environmental as well.

Still, researchers can hardly wait to get their hands on the gene in order to study just what it does. "It's very exciting," says Michael Bailey of Northwestern University in Chicago, co-author of a study two years ago that found half of the identical twins of gay men to be themselves gay. "If we can find a gene for sexual orientation, we can start to find out what the gene does."

The list of questions to be asked about the gene is endless: What protein does it code for? Where does this protein act and what does it do? How does the gene in homosexuals differ from the corresponding gene in heterosexual men? Does the gene invariably lead to homosexuality in males, or are there heterosexual males who also carry the gene? And what does the gene do in women?

REPLICATING STUDIES

First, however, the results must be replicated. Hamer, who has already begun collecting data for a follow-up, says he's confident this homosexuality link will stand up better than some of the earlier work that attempted to link behavioral conditions to particular chromosomes. Several of those studies fell apart when the diagnosis changed for one or two key individuals — when, for example, a subject who had previously shown no symptoms developed manic-depression. By including only homosexuals, Hamer doesn't have to worry about "false negatives" — males who claimed not to be homosexual but who really were. And the use of 40 separate families makes it less likely that a mis-characterization could skew the result. Furthermore, earlier studies often relied on incomplete genetic maps, while Hamer used 22 markers that covered the X chromosome.

Hamer gets a vote of confidence from geneticist Jeremy Nathans of Johns Hopkins University, who says that Hamer's methods should make the study "more robust" and less likely than earlier work to break down upon further inspection, although he, too, warns that it must be replicated.

Another factor that inspires confidence in other scientists is Hamer's reputation as a very careful worker. For much of the past decade he focused on the genes that code for metal-binding proteins, mostly in yeast and mice. "He could easily have stayed in that field and had a very distinguished career," Nathans says. Instead, Hamer says he "decided to work on something more general, more human," and settled on the issue of genes that affect sexual orientation.

FINDING THE GENE

Assuming that Hamer's linkage study does hold up as expected, he will find himself with another difficult problem on his hands — finding the male homosexuality gene that his data indicate is there, somewhere, in Xq28. It won't be easy. There are probably several hundred genes in that region, Hamer notes, most of them unidentified. The job will require assembling more and more families of homosexuals, analyzing the DNA with ever more markers, zeroing in on that one gene. And nobody has to tell Hamer that the search for the Huntington's disease gene, which finally ended earlier this year, dragged on for more than a decade after the gene had been traced to the tip of chromosome 4. But sooner or later, Hamer believes, someone will find this gene, and it might as well be him.

4   HOMOSEXUALITY AND BIOLOGY

GAY GENE STUDIES ARE IRRELEVANT

Charles Krauthammer

Charles Krauthammer wrote the following article for The Washington Post. *Krauthammer is a prominent journalist and national spokesperson for conservative ideas and causes.*

Points to Consider:

1. What do the twin studies imply about the incidence of homosexuality?

2. How might a society averse to homosexuality use the information about genetic disposition?

3. Why are gay activists eager for scientific proof of genetic disposition?

4. How might homosexuality be viewed in the same light as diabetes? As alcoholism?

Charles Krauthammer, "Science Does Not Belong in Policy on Homosexuality." © 1993, **The Washington Post** Writers Group. Reprinted with permission.

The fact is, however, that homosexuality will never be like race and gender, genetically speaking.

"Research Points Toward a 'Gay' Gene," announced *The Wall Street Journal*. This was one of the more restrained responses to the news coming out of the National Institutes of Health (NIH) that a new study of homosexuals had found that some might carry genes that might predispose them to homosexuality. *The New York Times* front page, gushing about "the politically explosive study of the origins of sexual orientation" noted that "the latest study is likely to add fuel to the debate over gay rights in the military and civilian realms."

If it does it will be another triumph of hype, another vivid demonstration of what can come from that volatile combination of scientific ignorance and journalistic sensationalism.

Twenty-five years ago that combination produced the widespread reporting of a genetic cause of criminality: the XYY (chromosomally abnormal) male. The link has since been discredited, most recently in a National Academy of Sciences study issued this year. We have also been treated to breathless reports of the discovery of genetic markers for alcoholism, manic-depression and schizophrenia. All these claims were subsequently retracted or refuted. The retractions, unlike the discoveries, tended not to make the front page.

This should be a caution that the "gay gene" may similarly not hold up. But even if it does, so what? The study shows that male sexual orientation may be influenced by a gene or genes at the tip of the X chromosome. That is scientifically interesting. But despite the hype, it has — or, at least, should have — no public policy implications.

Why not? If homosexuality is genetically determined like race and gender, then should it not be treated like race and gender as some immutable, accidental characteristic? Should it not then be welcomed as a normal condition of the human family, deserving guarantees and protection against any form of discrimination?

TWIN STUDIES

The fact is, however, that homosexuality will never be like race and gender, genetically speaking. Except in the rarest of cases, race and gender are entirely genetically determined. But we know from twin studies that the concordance rate of homosexuality in identical

GENETIC LINKS

The new study from the National Cancer Institute that purports to find "a genetic link to homosexuality" is interesting but inconclusive . . .

The study has a small sample size, and the participants in the "selected group" were recruited through advertisements in homosexual publications and through AIDS clinics, including the politically active Whitman-Walker Clinic in Washington, D.C. The subjects' homosexuality was assessed according to the "Kinsey Scale", an arbitrarily concocted measurement from the discredited studies of Alfred C. Kinsey. (Kinsey stated that only 4% of the population was heterosexual, with the rest being bisexual or homosexual, along a sliding scale rating heterosexuality as zero and homosexuality as 6.)

The researchers' biases are obvious from the start, when they define homosexuality as "a naturally occurring variation" of sexuality. Not all scientists accept the idea that homosexuality is "natural", and many dynamically oriented psychiatrists and psychotherapists believe that it is a condition that can be changed through therapy.

"New Genetic Study Not What It's Cracked Up to Be," **Family Research Council**, 1993

twins is only about 50 percent. Identical twins have identical genes. Yet if one twin is homosexual, half the time the other has the opposite sexual orientation.

That means that even giving the greatest benefit of the doubt to genetic factors, a huge source of homosexuality is nongenetic: environmental, behavioral, pedagogical. To put the twin study in perspective, the 50 percent concordance rate for homosexuality puts it somewhat below the concordance rate for manic-depressive disease — meaning that homosexuality is less "genetic" than the tendency to serious depression.

NEW STUDY

Moreover, the findings of the new "gay gene" study are far more modest than have been advertised. As the authors admit in the original article just published in *Science*, "At present, we can say nothing about the fraction of all instances of male homosexuality that are related or unrelated to the Xq28 (genetic) locus." All the study can say is that some males — we have no idea what percentage — may have a heightened genetic susceptibility to homosexuality.

But heightened genetic susceptibility occurs in dozens of common conditions. It is well known, for example, that obesity runs in families. Some people are genetically predisposed to getting fat. Now, if weight were 10 percent determined by genetics, that would have implications. If you were marked at birth for girth, you could go ahead and eat all the hot dogs you wanted, knowing that it would make no difference in the end.

But anything less than 100 percent genetic causation, and the environment comes into play. That is why it is extremely important what a person predisposed to obesity eats. If anything, a genetic predisposition makes it all the more important for a person to try to shape his environment and behavior to avoid his genetically preferred outcome. Similarly, a society averse to homosexuality might use this information about genetic predisposition for ever more stringent control of cultural influences and messages in the hope of "saving" the genetically predisposed from homosexuality.

SCIENCE, BEHAVIOR & MORALITY

That, of course, presupposes a society averse to homosexuality. Many gay activists entertain the hope that they can combat this aversion with scientific proof of a genetic basis for homosexuality. They try to draw on the prestige of science to justify homosexuality as a biologically determined and therefore normal human variant. The National Gay and Lesbian Task Force was out within minutes of the release of the gay gene study with a statement that "the NIH study...shows that homosexuality is a naturally occurring and common variation among humans."

Again, so what? So is diabetes. So is alcoholism. So is schizophrenia. Does that render any of these conditions desirable or normal? Does it tell us anything at all about how society ought to treat diabetics, alcoholics and schizophrenics?

Science has nothing to say to either side of the gay rights debate. The tolerance or discouragement of homosexuality is a question to be decided according to what people believe about the value, the morality, the chances for happiness of a homosexual life. The science is irrelevant. So is this study.

5 HOMOSEXUALITY AND BIOLOGY

HOMOSEXUAL BY BIRTH: THE POINT

John J. McNeill

Dr. John J. McNeill is a psychotherapist who was practicing in New York City when he wrote this article. McNeill is an independent scholar, lecturer and writer specializing in reflections on scripture in light of the gay experience.

Points to Consider:

1. What two-fold dilemma has been faced by the Christian gay community?

2. What is the implication of accepting sexual orientation as a "given", as with eye color?

3. Summarize McNeill's view of churches whose ministry is to help gay people lead celibate lives.

4. According to McNeill, how can homosexual love be holy love?

Human beings do not choose their sexual orientation; they discover it as something given.

It has been more than ten years since I wrote *The Church and the Homosexual*. . . Most importantly, I wrote the book because of my increasing awareness of the enormous amount of unjust suffering in the Christian gay community. I observed that many, if not most, lesbian women and homosexual men felt caught in a dilemma: to accept themselves and to affirm their sexuality, they believed that they must leave the church and even give up their faith; and to affirm their Christian faith, they felt they had to repress and deny their sexuality and lead a life devoid of any sexual intimacy. The evidence was clear to me that both solutions led to an unhappy and unhealthy life. I was convinced that what is bad psychologically has to be bad theologically and that, conversely, whatever is good theologically is certainly good psychologically. For as St. Irenaeus claimed, "The glory of God are humans fully alive."

NO DEVIATION

In *The Church and the Homosexual* I sought to overturn three traditional stances taken by the Christian community regarding lesbian and homosexual relationships. I opposed, first of all, the view that God intends all human beings to be heterosexual, and that therefore a failure to be heterosexual represents a deviation that demands an explanation, usually given in terms of sin or, more recently, in terms of sickness. According to this view, those who find themselves to be homosexual must change their orientation through prayer and counseling or, failing that, live totally chaste and sexually loveless lives. This is the position held in the Vatican letter "On the Pastoral Care of Homosexual Persons" issued to all the bishops of the world. This letter was deemed necessary to offset "deceitful propaganda" coming from gay Christian groups challenging the church's tradition and its interpretation of Scripture. According to this position, sexual fulfillment is exclusively the right of the heterosexual.

I proposed instead that God so created humans that they develop with a great variety of both gender identities and sexual-object choices. Consequently, the attempt to force humans into narrow heterosexist categories of what it means to be a man or a woman can destroy the great richness and variety of God's creation. Always and everywhere a certain percentage of men and women develop as homosexuals or lesbians. They should be considered as part of God's creative plan. Their sexual orientation has no necessary connection with sin, sickness or failure; rather, it is a gift from God to be accepted and lived out with gratitude. God does not despise anything that God has created.

NO CHOICE

It should be stressed here, in opposition to certain current views, that human beings do not choose their sexual orientation; they discover it as something given. To pray for a change in sexual orientation is about as meaningful as to pray for a change from blue eyes to brown. Furthermore, there is no healthy way to reverse or change sexual orientation once it is established. The claim of certain groups to be able to change homosexuals into heterosexuals has been shown to be spurious and frequently based on homophobia (cf. Ralph Blair's pamphlet "Ex-Gay" [HCCC Inc., 1982]). The usual technique used to bring about this pseudo-change involves helping gay persons internalize self-hatred, an approach that frequently causes great psychological harm and suffering. The Christian communities that make use of this sort of ministry usually do so to avoid any challenge to their traditional attitude and to avoid any dialogue with self-accepting gays and truly professional psychotherapists. (The psychotherapists whom these churches frequently cite are generally very conservative and homophobic in their orientation.) The real choice that faces lesbians and homosexuals is not between heterosexuality and homosexuality but between a homosexual relationship or no relational intimacy whatsoever.

Other churches have confined their official ministries to helping gay people live out celibate lives. According to Christian tradition, celibacy is a special gift of God given to a certain few for the sake of the kingdom. The occasional homosexual who receives this gift is, indeed, blessed. Clergy choose a celibate lifestyle voluntarily, but gay people are given no choice; they are told they must live celibate lives. But there is no reason to believe that God grants this gift to everyone who is lesbian or homosexual. On the contrary, empirical studies have shown that the vast majority of gay people who have attempted a celibate lifestyle end up acting out their sexual needs in promiscuous and self-destructive ways. Every human being has a God-given right to sexual love and intimacy. Anyone who would deny this right to any individual must prove without a doubt the grounds for this denial. The only healthy and holy Christian response to a homosexual orientation is to learn to accept it and live it out in a way that is consonant with Christian values.

ATTENTION: STATE LEGISLATURE! DO NOT PROTECT THE RIGHTS OF HOMOSEXUALS!

RIGHT WING RELIGIOUS LOBBY

HIS MASTER'S VOICE

Cartoon by Bill Sanders. Reprinted with permission of **The Milwaukee Journal**.

NOT A MENACE

The second thesis of my book was that homosexuals, rather than being somehow a menace to the values of society and the family, as Christians have tended to assume, have, as a part of God's creative plan, special gifts and qualities and a very positive contribution to make to the development of society (cf. also my article "Homosexuality, Lesbianism, and the Future: The Creative Role of the Gay Community in Building a More Humane Society," in *A Challenge to Love: Gay and Lesbian Catholics in the Church*, edited by Robert Nugent [Crossroad, 1984]). Indeed, if lesbians and homosexuals were to disappear, the further development of society toward greater humanness could be seriously endangered. Consequently, I am convinced that there is a special providence in the emergence of visible gay communities within the Christian churches at this point in history.

A HOLY LOVE

The third thesis of my book was perhaps the most controversial. The traditional position has been that since every homosexual act is sinful and contrary to God's plan, the love that exists between gay

> # HOMOSEXUAL GENES
>
> *A predisposition for homosexuality appears to be written into the very genes of some men. And they get the key genes from their mothers.*
>
> Kim Painter, "Key Evidence: More Maternal Kin Are Gay," **USA Today**, July 16, 1993

people is a sinful love which alienates the lovers from God. I argued that the love between two lesbians or two homosexuals, assuming that it is a constructive human love, is not sinful nor does it alienate the lovers from God's plan, but can be a holy love, mediating God's presence in the human community as effectively as heterosexual love.

I fully appreciated how controversial my arguments were. But I pointed out that there was new evidence — from biblical studies and from various empirical studies in the human sciences, especially psychology and sociology — that completely undermined the traditional understanding of homosexuality as a chosen and changeable state. Examples of recent psychological data come from new insights into psychosexual development, e.g., (a) one has no choice about sexual orientation; (b) the only healthy reaction to being homosexual is to accept it. And, above all else, there was new evidence coming from the collective experience of lesbians and homosexuals who as committed Christians were seeking to live their lives in conformity with Christian faith and Christian values. All this evidence should give every Christian community serious reason to reconsider its understanding of homosexuality. . .

Only a sadistic God would create hundreds of thousands of humans to be inherently homosexual and then deny them the right to sexual intimacy. I, for one, would prefer to believe that the church is wrong about homosexual activity than that this sadistic, super-ego God has any true relation to the God of love revealed by Jesus.

Conservative and fundamentalist churches, for their part, also do not engage in moral debate. They feel that they have a clear and direct revelation of God's will concerning homosexuality, and they vigorously condemn it on the basis of biblical fundamentalism and a conservative acceptance of certain cultural mores, especially in the sexual realm (such as the dominance of men over women). . .

CONCLUSION

There can be no valid moral debate on these issues that does not include lesbian and gay people as full participants. The Holy Spirit has something to say to the churches in and through the experience of lesbian and homosexual Christians. A truly extraordinary witness to the kind of full human love that can exist between two gay persons is being manifested daily by AIDS victims and their lovers and friends. The exceptional fidelity, self-sacrifice and affection, as well as the pain, grief and sorrow and the deep spiritual response to the suffering and bereavement that is being expressed, is a sign to the churches of the presence of the Spirit of love in these relationships. "See how they love one another!"

6 | HOMOSEXUALITY AND BIOLOGY

HOMOSEXUAL BY BIRTH: THE COUNTERPOINT

Sy Rogers and Alan Medinger

Sy Rogers and Alan Medinger wrote the following article for Exodus International, *a world-wide network of Christian organizations which minister to those overcoming homosexuality and life-dominating sexual problems.*

Points to Consider:

1. How do Rogers and Medinger counter the statement "They're born gay"?

2. Discuss: "If the patients are motivated…a large percentage will give up their homosexuality."

3. Summarize arguments for considering homosexuality a mental disorder.

4. Explain the theory of "same-sex deficit".

Sy Rogers and Alan Medinger, "Homosexuality and the Truth." © 1990, 1991 by **Exodus International**, P.O. Box 2121, San Rafael, CA 94912. Reprinted with permission.

"The genetic theory of homosexuality has been generally discarded today."

For many years the politically active segment of the gay community has effectively used the media as a means to change society's attitudes about homosexuality. In some ways, this has been helpful in curbing mistreatment of homosexuals. However, for the purpose of social "legitimization" of homosexuality (attained through political and religious systems), the gay community has also disseminated much questionable information.

They have attempted to convince society that homosexuality is innate, unchangeable and a normal variable in the spectrum of human sexuality. If this is true, then homosexuals would be deserving of minority status, entitled to the rights and protection of other legitimate minority groups. Rather than speculate on what that could mean, let's instead ask if the pro-homosexual message is based on truth. Are their claims legitimate? The following is a compilation of responses to the most common pro-gay arguments.

1) "Some people are meant to be gay — they're born gay."

Nothing has been published and gained wide acceptance in the scientific and medical communities to indicate that homosexuality is primarily genetic or otherwise prenatally determined. One of the most widely recognized authorities on the subject is John W. Money, Ph.D., a professor at the Johns Hopkins School of Medicine, and Director of the Psychohormonal Research Institute. In an article in *Perspectives in Human Sexuality*, he states: "Whatever may be the possible unlearned assistance from constitutional sources, the child's psychosexual identity is not written, unlearned, in the genetic code, the hormonal system or the nervous system at birth."[1]

A psychiatrist who has written and spoken widely on the subject of homosexuality, Dr. Charles W. Socarides, of the Albert Einstein College of Medicine in New York, says this: "Homosexuality, the choice of a partner of the same sex for orgastic satisfaction, is not innate. There is no connection between sexual instinct and the choice of sexual object. Such an object choice is learned, acquired behavior; there is no inevitable genetically inborn propensity toward the choice of a partner of either the same or opposite sex."[2]

Finally we have the opinions of Masters and Johnson, the most widely-known authorities in the field of human sexual behavior. In one of their books, they write: "The genetic theory of homosexuality has been generally discarded today. Despite the interest in possible hormone mechanisms in the origin of homosexuality, no serious scientist today suggests that a simple cause-effect relationship applies."[3]

2) "Homosexuals can't change — and to suggest they try is unrealistic, even harmful."

Again, some of the most prominent specialists in this field disagree. Dr. Reuben Fine, director for the New York Center for Psychoanalytic Training, says in his 1987 publication, *Psychoanalytic Theory, Male and Female Homosexuality: Psychological Approaches:* "I have recently had occasion to review the result of psychotherapy with homosexuals, and been surprised by the finds. It is paradoxical that even though politically active homosexual groups deny the possibility of change, all studies from

Schrenck-Notzing on have found positive effects, virtually regardless of the kind of treatment used...a considerable percentage of overt homosexuals became heterosexual...If the patients were motivated, whatever procedure is adopted, a large percentage will give up their homosexuality..."

3) "Homosexuality is no longer considered a mental disorder."

The gay community claimed a great victory when they prevailed upon the American Psychiatric Association (APA) to remove homosexuality from the DSM-II, its listing of psychological disorders. This highly controversial action seems to fly in the face of the evidence of any common-sense definition of psychological well-being. Consider the following: Homosexual men are six times more likely to have attempted suicide than heterosexual men.[4]

Studies indicate that between 25 and 33% of homosexual men and women are alcoholics,[5] compared to a 7% figure for the general population.[6] Statistics give evidence of widespread sexual compulsion among homosexual men. A major Kinsey study revealed that 43% of the homosexual men surveyed estimated that they had had sex with 500 or more partners; 28% with 1,000 or more partners.[7]

Either the APA is ignorant of what homosexuality entails for vast numbers of men, or their view of healthy sexuality indicates a serious disorder among members of the APA. The same Kinsey study revealed that homosexual men have to a great extent separated sexuality from relationship. The survey showed 79% of the respondents saying that over half of their sexual partners were strangers. Seventy percent said that over half of their sexual partners were people with whom they had sex only once.[8] Surely this is an indication of either deep dissatisfaction, or else terribly destructive hedonism...

4) "I didn't choose to be gay."

"The homosexual has no choice as regards his or her sexual object," says Dr. Charles Socarides. "The condition is unconsciously determined, is differentiated from the behavior of a person who deliberately engages in same-sex sexual contact due to situational factors or a desire for variational experiences.

"As noted above, these constitute non-clinical forms of homosexual behavior. The nuclear core of true homosexuality is never a conscious choice, an act of will; but rather it is determined from the earliest period of childhood, in terms of origin of course, not in practice."[9]

SAME-SEX DEFICIT

Dr. Elizabeth Moberly of Cambridge, England, author of two clinical books regarding origins and treatment of homosexuality, believes that it is important to see the homosexual condition as involving a same-sex developmental deficit, resulting in an insecure identity which cripples same-sex relationships. Due to some early difficulty, especially with the same-sex parent — such as separation or emotional unavailability — there remains an unmet need for love and identification, together with a half-hidden sense of hurt or grievance, toward members of the same sex.

Dr. Moberly believes the path toward growth and change requires a same-sex therapist, who will help the homosexual to build a more secure identity through fulfilling legitimate relational needs in healthy non-sexual ways, and through resolving same-sex hurts and conflicts from the past. Dr. Moberly concludes that realistic heterosexual relating becomes possible when same-sex issues have been addressed.

CONCLUSION

We recognize that many are content to pursue their homosexual orientation and the related lifestyle. However, many other homosexually-oriented persons do not wish to have their lives defined or determined by this inclination.

 We live in a nation famous for our premise of self-determination. Those who are unhappy with their homosexuality have the right to explore their clinically-valid option of impulse control and orientational change.

ENDNOTES

[1] John W. Money, "Sexual Dimorphism and Homosexual Gender Identity," in **Perspectives in Human Sexuality**, ed. Nathaniel W. Wagner (New York: Behavioral Publications, 1974), p. 67.

[2] Charles W. Socarides, "Homosexuality: Basic Concepts and Psychodynamics," in the **International Journal of Psychiatry**, 1972.

[3] William H. Masters, Virginia E. Brown, and Robert C. Kolodny, **Human Sexuality** (Boston: Little, Brown and Company, 1984), pp. 319-20.

[4] Alan Bell and Martin Weinberg, **Homosexualities: A Study of Diversities Among Men and Women** (Simon & Schuster, 1978), Table 21.12.

5 Robert J. Kus, "Alcoholics Anonymous and Gay American Men," **Journal of Homosexuality**, Vol. 14, No. 2 (1987), p. 254.

6 Interview with staff at an alcoholic treatment center in San Rafael, CA; November, 1990

7 Bell and Weinberg, **Homosexualities**, p. 308.

8 Ibid., pp. 308-309.

9 Charles W. Socarides, "Sexual Politics, Scientific Logic: The Issue of Homosexuality," **Hope for Homosexuality**, p. 57.

EXAMINING COUNTERPOINTS

This activity may be used as an individualized study guide for students in libraries and resource centers or as a discussion catalyst in small group and classroom discussions.

The Point

Most homosexuals are born with a same-sex biological orientation.

The Counterpoint

There is no reliable scientific evidence that homosexuality has a genetic basis.

• • • •

The Point

Scientific evidence that homosexuality has a genetic basis would not be a reason to condone or promote homosexual behavior.

The Counterpoint

If there is a gay gene and people cannot control preference any more than skin color, special civil rights protection in law must be extended to homosexuals.

• • • •

The Point

Homosexuals must change their orientation through prayer and counseling.

The Counterpoint

There is no theological or psychological need for homosexuals to change their orientation.

The Point

"Homosexual acts are sinful and contrary to God's plan. Love that exists between gay people is a sinful love which alienates the lovers from God." (Locate the reading for this quote in Chapter One.)

The Counterpoint

"Love between two lesbians or two gays, assuming that it is constructive human love, is not sinful nor does it alienate the lovers from God's plan. It can be a holy love, reflecting God's presence as effectively as heterosexual love." (Locate the reading for this quote in Chapter One.)

Guidelines

Part A

Examine the counterpoints above and then consider the following questions.

1. Do you agree more with the point or counterpoint in each case? Why?

2. Which reading in this publication best illustrates the point in each case?

3. Which reading best illustrates each counterpoint?

Part B

Social issues are usually complex, but often problems become oversimplified in political debates and discussions. Usually a polarized version of social conflict does not adequately represent the diversity of views that surround social conflict. Examine the counterpoints above. Then write down other possible interpretations.

CHAPTER 2

HOMOSEXUALITY AND RELIGION

7   HOMOSEXUALITY AND RELIGION

THE CHURCH AND HOMOSEXUALITY: AN OVERVIEW

Brian Jaudon

Brian Jaudon wrote the following article for Sojourners, *a religious magazine that reflects on social, moral and political issues in relation to the gospel.*

Points to Consider:

1. Describe the church distinction between "orientation" and "practice".

2. What is the "starting point" for Christian social activists in their struggle with the gay issue?

3. Explain the moral implications of "driving a wedge between love-making and procreation".

4. Why are the church leaders so hesitant to enter into dialogue on the gay issue?

Brian Jaudon, "Churches Struggle to Address Homosexuality," **Sojourners**, July 1991. Reprinted by permission.

Until the church is of a "common mind" on these questions — if it ever will be — the dialogue will no doubt be long and often painful.

Most mainline denominations and the Catholic Church acknowledge in official church statements that most gays and lesbians are homosexual by "orientation" and not by choice. While advocating for the full civil rights of gays and lesbians, and affirming them as "children of God" or "individuals of sacred worth", most stop short of condoning or accepting the "practice" of homosexuality. In other words, the church generally calls on gays and lesbians to be celibate, along with non-married heterosexuals.

ORIENTATION AND PRACTICE

This distinction between "orientation" and "practice" has been a helpful one to many, including gays and lesbians who have been unable to reconcile their sexuality with what they believe God intended in creating humans male and female. But gays and lesbians who fully embrace their same-sex orientation experience the distinction between orientation and practice as little more than a euphemistic rejection cloaked in affirming language.

"In real life, those who are not called to be celibate try to integrate their sexuality with physical expressions of it," says Father Robert Nugent, a Catholic priest who has been involved in gay and lesbian ministry for the past 20 years. "Gay people feel if you can't support this expression, which is God's gift to me, then you're not supporting me as a person."

"Why should people with a homosexual orientation not live out that orientation and express their full being, just as heterosexuals are able to do so?" asks Rev. Kit Cherry, a field director of the Universal Fellowship of Metropolitan Community Church, a denomination founded in 1968 as a welcoming place for gays and lesbians.

That is one of the most difficult theological and pastoral questions facing the communities of faith today — and for the foreseeable future. And the way it is answered is certain to have profound implications for the church.

TRADITIONAL STANCE

For some theologians and laypersons who take a more traditional stance toward homosexuality — and sexual ethics in general —

than the authors of the Presbyterian report, the issues seem clear. "The scriptures are much clearer on this issue than many people claim," Ron Sider, of Evangelicals for Social Action, told *Sojourners*. "It is contrary to biblical teaching to endorse the practice of homosexuality."

Others anguish over the issue but still cannot fully affirm gay sexuality. "It is clear, to me at least, that God in creation intended and intends our sexual lives to be lived out heterosexually," Lewis Smedes told *Sojourners*. "What many gay people want to hear is that being gay is simply another version of sexuality."

"I'm in the position — and I cannot logically escape it — that homosexuality is a tragedy more than a moral failure. This stance is very unsatisfying to my gay friends. I can't undo that. If I discovered one of my own children were gay, I would consider that cause for sadness and regret. But I would not love them less. In fact, I would probably love them more. And I would be contentious in demanding that their condition not rob them of any justice.

"When gays live together in a seriously committed relationship, I thank God that they have that kind of relationship. It may be the best possible under the circumstances. I cannot find it in myself to condemn it. But if the church publicly blesses it, it blesses a partnership that isn't a marriage."

SOCIAL ACTIVISTS

Many Christian social activists are struggling with this issue as well. "I have to declare myself an agnostic regarding the question of whether homosexuality was part of God's plan in creation," confessed Ken Sehested, of the Baptist Peace Fellowship. "I would give anything to be able to give a clear, unequivocal answer. But I simply don't know. What I do know, and know very clearly, is that I've become acquainted with gay men and lesbian women who both profess and live gospel values as much or more so than I do, and who continue to teach me about God's presence.

"There may be genuine theological disagreement — disagreement that is not rooted in homophobia — but at the very least, the church must put the weight of its influence behind civil rights for gays and lesbians."

MAINLINE CHURCHES

With so many in the church clearly wrestling with their own convictions about homosexuality, a few mainline Protestant denominations are in the process of reviewing their policies toward gays and lesbians in the church.

The stakes are high. As the special task forces continue to sort through the different biblical scholarship as well as recent sociological and physiological evidence pertaining to homosexuality, some churches have threatened to leave their respective denominations if gay sexuality is ever affirmed in their church. Meanwhile, more and more gays and lesbians in the church are becoming increasingly weary of this discussion altogether.

"My tolerance for debating whether I am sinful or sick by virtue of being homosexual has, after 16 years before the mast, reached nil," wrote Episcopalian John Fortunato in a recent issue of *Christianity and Crisis*, after resigning from his eighth church committee on sexuality in the past 14 years. "If the church needs to continue its 'tempest in a tabernacle' about sexuality for another 150 years, so be it. But I have no energy for it."

ORDINATION

The ordination of non-celibate gays and lesbians appears to be where the political battle lines have been drawn in the homosexuality debate among mainline Protestant churches. . .

A political storm followed the ordination of J. Robert Williams — an openly practicing gay man — in Hoboken, New Jersey, on December 16, 1989. Billed by the diocese of New Jersey as the "second openly homosexual person to be ordained in the Episcopal Church," the Williams ordination was seen by many as a public challenge by New Jersey Bishop John Spong to the denomination's intended policy against ordaining practicing gays and lesbians...

46

THE CHURCH

If the church is going to have any kind of fruitful dialogue on issues relating to sexual ethics, the structure and tone will need to change, according to many participants in the discussion.

"Though many people are pleading for a dialogue, the main voices don't appear to be open to listening to each other," says Philip Turner, professor of ethics at General Theological Seminary in New York City. "It's contending parties — not dialogue — whose positions are articulated largely without reference to the concerns of the other party.

"More conservative forces have not taken seriously what is involved pastorally with respect to asking those not married to abstain from sexual relations and the egregious treatment of single people and gay people. On the other hand, advocates of a new ethic haven't addressed two questions: What are the moral implications of, in principle, driving a wedge between lovemaking and procreation? And what do commitment and faithfulness mean? When pressed, there is not an adequate response to these. The revisionists have not made their case in my mind.

"Both sides are creating an environment of terror. Anyone making moderate overtures is jumped on. I know colleagues who don't want to write on this subject out of fear of being vilified. If you argue against the position of revising the stand on gays, you are called homophobic; there is a huge price to be paid. And the vast middle is afraid to enter the debate because they fear being called intolerant..."

Many of those interviewed for this article stressed the importance of keeping the dialogue on a personal level, by getting to know gays and lesbians rather than dealing with the issue simply in the abstract. "We do better talking about sexual ethics as long as we keep it theoretical and sterile," says Sally Brown Geis, a sociologist on the faculty of Iliff Seminary in Denver and a member of the United Methodist study committee. "But we're not intellectualizing about some theory; we're talking about people's lives..."

Until the church is of a "common mind" on these questions — if it ever will be — the dialogue will no doubt be long and often painful. But as one observer noted, we have much to learn from each other in the meantime.

8 HOMOSEXUALITY AND RELIGION

TO LICENSE A GAY MINISTER

Keith Hartman

Keith Hartman is a free-lance writer living in Durham, North Carolina. He wrote this article for Christian Social Action, *a journal of social, moral, political and religious reflection, published by the General Board of Church and Society of The United Methodist Church.*

Points to Consider:

1. Describe John Blevins' struggle with his sexuality.

2. How did Blevins answer the challenge about being a good role model for children?

3. How did Blevins' licensing as a minister affect the entire Southwestern Baptist Convention?

Keith Hartman, "To License a Gay Minister," **Christian Social Action**, November 1992. Reprinted with permission.

The Southern Baptist Church used to cite Scripture to prove that enslavement of blacks was a moral practice.

On April 5, 1992, members of a small Southern Baptist congregation chose to take a costly ethical stand. That night they affirmed that an openly gay member of their congregation had a sincere calling to the ministry, and they awarded him a license to preach the gospel. This decision placed the church in direct conflict with the fundamentalist leaders of the Southern Baptist Convention, which, within two months, expelled the church.

The mainstream press covered Binkley Memorial Baptist Church's expulsion in great detail. It was, after all, the first time a church had ever been kicked out of the Southern Baptist Convention. The public was treated to a barrage of quotes from worried ministers and zealous delegates.

However, even with all this reporting, we've managed to miss completely the important part of this story. We've listened to a lot of outsiders debate the rightness or wrongness of Binkley's position, but no one has ever explained how Binkley came to make that fateful decision in the first place. What led a small Southern Baptist church to license a gay minister?

Actually, the episode started more than a year ago. That's when John Blevins, a divinity student at Duke University, was presented to the deacons of Binkley Memorial Baptist in Chapel Hill, North Carolina, as a candidate to be licensed to preach the gospel. Licensing, the first step in becoming a Baptist minister, requires the approval of the candidate's congregation and represents its belief in his sincerity and commitment to the ministry. Usually, it is a routine procedure, taking a couple of weeks to process. But then usually the candidate isn't an openly gay man who has been talking honestly with the congregation about his sexuality.

A SINCERE CALL TO MINISTRY

The deacons who interviewed John were united in finding that he had a sincere calling to the ministry. However, they were divided over the role that his sexuality should play in their decision. Some felt that John's homosexuality made him inherently unsuitable for the ministry; others said that if God had truly called John, then God's will must be accepted and respected. In the end, the deacons arrived at a typically Baptist solution.

In the Baptist Church each individual church is autonomous and democratic; beliefs and policy aren't handed down from some outside authority. Instead, each congregation debates its own problems and votes on how to handle them.

The deacons at Binkley decided that, rather than voting blindly on the issue, they would take several months to educate themselves and the congregation about John's situation...The congregation thought a lot about these issues during those months, and, finally, on a rainy night in January, the members called on John to answer their questions himself.

"SOMETHING I HAD TO DO"

John began by telling the congregation about the summer after his junior year in high school, when he first felt his calling to the ministry. He was at church camp, and he remembers feeling, "something happening...something I needed to do, something I had to do, something I ought to do."

At the time, he told no one about this feeling. He knew that emotions often run high at church summer camps, and that many of his friends would make promises then on which they would never follow through. He didn't know if his own commitment would outlast the summer, but it turned out to be a feeling that never left him.

John also told the congregation about his struggle with his sexuality. By the time he received the calling, John had already realized he was attracted to men. He talked about his fear and his frustration at not being able to ask anyone for help. John spoke of the times that he prayed to God to remove this attraction, to heal him. He also spoke of the time, years later, when he finally came to accept it, to see it as a natural part of himself. He told them he came to

50

realize that God hadn't "fixed" it because it was never something broken in the first place.

Some members of the congregation asked John about the biblical prohibitions on homosexual acts. John answered them by pointing to times in the past when Scripture had been used to justify unjust behavior. The Southern Baptist Church used to cite Scripture to prove that enslavement of blacks was a moral practice. Some Southern Baptists still use passages from the Bible to argue that women should be subjugated to their men. John asked: Should we accept these interpretations, and go back to the days of slavery? Or should we instead take a look at what is going on in our world, and ask how a loving and fair God would have us act? Should we respond with compassion or with bigotry?

A GOOD ROLE MODEL?

Another member of the congregation asked if John thought that a gay minister could be a good role model for children. John answered the unspoken part of the question by saying that he didn't think that seeing a gay minister would lead a child toward becoming homosexual. "After all, a heterosexual minister didn't cause me to be straight," he said.

However, John also pointed out that the congregation would need to accept the fact that some of its children are going to grow up to be gay. Therefore, having a gay minister to talk with, and a church which accepts them, might make those children's lives a whole lot easier — particularly when they are coming to terms with their sexuality and how to use it responsibly.

Some other members were more concerned about how licensing John would affect Binkley. They pointed out that one deacon had already left the church, and they expressed their fear that other members might do the same. They asked John if his licensing was really worth the division it was causing in the church.

John responded by saying that the division on the issue of homosexuality had been there long before he had ever joined Binkley. He was simply bringing it to the surface, where it could be discussed, debated and, he hoped, healed. "The church has got to deal with this issue," he said. "It's not going to go away. There are a lot of people who already feel alienated from the church. Will we reach out to them or take the easy route by denying them?"

A LICENSE TO PREACH

A week after that meeting, the deacons met to render their verdict: one of them abstained from the process; seven of them voted against John's licensing; 15 of them affirmed it and recommended John to the lay members.

A month later, on April 5, the congregation as a whole gathered to make their final decision. After hours of debate, they finally cast their vote; a majority of 57.5 percent expressed their faith in John. That evening he was at last awarded a license to preach the gospel.

Since that action Binkley has faced difficult times. Other Southern Baptists, outraged by such a blatant support of homosexuality, moved to censure the Binkley action. On June 9, the Southern Baptist Convention expelled the entire congregation from the fold. On the same day, the Convention struck down the long-standing Baptist tradition of autonomous churches and began issuing decrees of faith. From now on, the Convention declared, all Southern Baptists must accept opposition to homosexuality as part of their creed.

Binkley isn't particularly affected by this action; it has been financially independent from the Convention for years. The seven deacons who opposed John's licensing have left for another church, but the majority of the lay members have remained. As Linda Jordan, the head minister, said, "We were trying to make an honest decision, and we will now take whatever consequences that entails."

As for John — he got a job with an American Baptist Church up in Chicago, so he left North Carolina in August. Sometime before he departed, he described the flood of mail that he got from other gay Southern Baptists. Most of them are too closeted to speak out, but they seem to feel they have found some voice in John. Who knows, maybe in a few years they will be ready to speak for themselves — and maybe in a few years, their churches will even be ready to listen.

9   HOMOSEXUALITY AND RELIGION

HOMOSEXUAL MINISTERS SHOULD NOT BE ORDAINED

Presbyterian Minority Report on Human Sexuality

The following article is excerpted from the Presbyterian Minority Report on Human Sexuality. This report appears in the minutes of the 203rd General Assembly of the Presbyterian Church (U.S.A.).

Points to Consider:

1. Briefly summarize the Presbyterian stance on the practice of homosexuality.

2. How does the Presbyterian Church explain its readiness to welcome homosexuals as members?

3. Explain: "Sexual orientation, in itself, is not a barrier to ordination."

4. How should ordination of self-declared, openly practicing homosexuals be viewed by the church?

"Minority Report on Human Sexuality," 203rd General Assembly Minutes of the Presbyterian Church (USA), 1991. Reprinted with permission.

In the act of ordaining, the church would then be sanctioning homosexual practice.

The English word "homosexual" is of relatively modern origin, having first been used, it seems, about 1890. It is made up of two words, namely *homo*, a Greek word meaning "same", and *sexualis*, a late Latin word referring to sex or the sexes. "Homosexual", therefore, is literally "same-sex", and refers to sexual activity of male with male, or female with female.

THE BIBLE

Naturally the original documents of the Bible do not use this modern term, but it does not follow that the biblical writers were unacquainted with those who indulged in homosexual practices. The occurrence of same-sex activities in the ancient Near-Eastern cultures and, still more, in the Greco-Roman empire, was notorious, and both Old Testament and New Testament writers are forthright in condemning such practices. The following is a brief summary of biblical passages that refer to homosexual practices. In order, however, to appreciate fully the import of the scriptural condemnation of homosexual practices, it will be helpful to glance at the total picture of human sexuality as set forth in the Old and New Testaments...

The life-long commitment of husband and wife to each other is emphasized again and again in both testaments. Not only the Old Testament commandment against committing adultery, a commandment repeated in the New Testament, but also such narratives as those that tell of Joseph resisting the impure advances of Potiphar's wife (Gen. 39), the sin of David with Bathsheba (2 Sam. 11), Hosea's distress occasioned by the continuing unfaithfulness of his wife Gomer, the words of Jesus concerning the lustful gaze of man upon a woman (Matt. 5:28), the admonition in the Letter to the Hebrews that the marriage bed be kept undefiled, "for God will judge fornicators and adulterers" (Heb. 13:4) — all these passages unite in describing the kind of relationship that God intends to be normative for a man and a woman.

Within this pattern of consistent emphasis on the purity of the marriage relationship between husband and wife, it is not surprising that the Bible condemns homosexual practices as unacceptable deviations from God's intention for humankind. In the Old Testament the Holiness Code of Leviticus specifically declares, "You shall not lie with a male as with a woman; it is an abomination" (Lev. 18:22). In fact, the punishment prescribed for such practice is death; "If a man lies with a male as with a woman, both of them have committed an abomination; they shall be put to death; their blood is upon them" (Lev. 20:13)...

NEW TESTAMENT

In the New Testament several writers refer to same-sex practices as reprehensible and contrary to God's intention for humankind. In his correspondence with the church at Corinth the Apostle Paul declares: "Fornicators, adulterers, male prostitutes, sodomites, thieves, the greedy, drunkards, revilers, robbers — none of these will inherit the kingdom of God" (1 Cor. 6:9-10). Here the Greek words that the New Revised Standard Version renders "male prostitutes" and "sodomites" (malakoi; arsenokoitai) refer to the passive and active partners respectively in male homosexual relations. (James Moffatt's translation uses the more technical phraseology "atamites and sodomites".)

In his letter to the Romans (Rom. 1:26-27) Paul broadens his condemnation of homosexual practices by including also sexual activities of women with women (often called "lesbianism"). The same condemnation against sodomites is repeated again in the first letter to Timothy (1 Tim. 1:10), a letter often considered today to have been written by a follower of Paul after Paul's death. If this is so, it broadens still further the basis of the witness of the New Testament against same-sex practices. Two of the shorter letters in the New Testament refer to the men of Sodom as examples of unbridled licentiousness (2 Pet. 2:6-7) and unnatural lust (Jude 7)...

HOMOSEXUALS

It is clear, according to the General Assembly's decision in 1978, that homosexual persons are to be welcomed into church membership. That decision reads:

Persons who manifest homosexual behavior must be treated with the profound respect and pastoral tenderness due all people of God...Homosexual persons are encompassed by the searching love of Christ...As persons repent and believe they become members of Christ's body. The church is not a citadel of the morally perfect; it is a hospital for sinners. It is the fellowship where contrite, needy people rest their hope for salvation on Christ and his righteousness. Here in community they seek and receive forgiveness and new life.

The church must become the nurturing community so that all those whose lives come short of the glory of God are converted, reoriented and built up into Christian maturity. It may be only in the context of loving community, appreciation, pastoral care, forgiveness and nurture that homosexual persons can come to a clear understanding of God's pattern for their sexual expression.

ORDINATION

Now, concerning the question of ordination: The 1978 policy statement was a response to Overture 9 (1976) asking "definitive guidance in regard to the ordination of persons who may be otherwise well-qualified but who affirm their own homosexual identity and practice." The General Assembly decision speaks of "self-affirming, practicing homosexual persons". The operative clause reads: "That unrepentant homosexual practice does not accord with the requirements for ordinations set forth in the Book of Order. . ."

We believe that the decision of 1978, with respect to ordination, concerns itself solely with homosexual practice and not with orientation, as such. Indeed, the decision deals with "self-affirming" or "unrepentant" practice. Sexual orientation, in itself, is not a barrier to ordination...The question of the ordination of self-affirming, practicing homosexual persons is indeed a moral question: Is the church to approve homosexual practice?

Terry Anderson, Professor of Christian Ethics, Vancouver School of Theology, United Church of Canada, says:

"Who and what is acceptable to the church for its spiritual and moral leadership indicates clearly some of the matter about which the church feels strongly. This may not have anything to do with different standards for ordained ministry and general membership. It does have to do with the public visibility and the degree of scrutiny, accountability and discipline the church demands. This is why the ordination, rather than the membership of homosexual persons is the focus of controversy."

The sanctioning function is also why the deliberate act of ordaining self-declared, practicing homosexual persons is seen in a particular light. To ordain such persons would be a powerful act of sanction. To ordain self-affirming, practicing homosexual persons would be to resolve the moral question of homosexual practice. In the act of ordaining, the church would then be sanctioning homosexual practice.

MORAL ISSUES

It is, no doubt, true that a large, diverse national church such as ours has great difficulty dealing with moral issues, particularly moral questions related to sexuality. And we may, therefore, be tempted to substitute a polity (political) decision for a moral decision. One way of resolving the moral question of homosexual practice by means of polity (church politics) would be for the church to determine that the question of who will be ordained will be a matter for presbyteries to decide in the case of ministers, for congregations to decide in the case of elders and deacons, and that these decisions would no longer be subject to definitive guidance. If we were to take this course, we would be inviting a particular part of the church to commit the whole church to a new set of moral standards, without the whole church deliberately "sitting under the Word" and testing this major change that affects the lives of all and pertains to our faithfulness as the church of Jesus Christ.

We would also be encouraging different parts of the church to go in different ways, and thus bringing further disconnection to our church. And we would be saying that this matter of sexual moral standards is inconsequential for the life of the church, a course we have been willing to take on another crucial contemporary issue, the ordination of women.

We believe, therefore, that the church's present stance of welcoming homosexual persons into the church and not ordaining "self-affirming, practicing homosexual persons" is consistent with the understanding of membership and with our understanding of the scriptural teaching with regard to homosexual practice.

10   HOMOSEXUALITY AND RELIGION

HOMOSEXUALITY AND THE BIBLE: THE POINT

The Plough

The following article appeared in The Plough. *It is published by the Plough Publishing House of the Hutterian Brethren Service Committee.* The Plough *is dedicated to all who work for a personal transformation in Christ and a radical turn from the materialism, militarism, racism, and impurity of this world, looking toward the coming of God's kingdom.*

Points to Consider:

1. Summarize arguments that might be used as proof that homosexuality is unnatural.

2. Briefly describe the agenda of the gay rights movement.

3. What might be seen as the role of the Christian toward the "repentant" homosexual?

4. Discuss: "The worst evil of the gay liberation movement is that it deprives homosexuals of any possible victory..."

"No One Calls It Sin Anymore," **The Plough**, February-March, 1993. Reprinted with permission.

Homosexuality is not only a violation of the law of God, but as Paul states, it is also unnatural.

Virtually the first official action taken by President Bill Clinton on his assumption of office was to direct the Department of Defense to reverse its long-standing policy of prohibiting homosexuals from serving in the military. Since Mr. Clinton has clearly allied himself with the gay liberation movement, this will certainly not be the last time he uses his powers as President to promote the agenda of the gay activists. Meanwhile in New York, school boards are coming under increasing pressure to accept curricula which promote homosexuality as a normal, even desirable "alternative lifestyle". According to a recent issue of *Time*, even first-graders are to be exposed to such books as *My Daddy's Roommate* (in which two smiling men are portrayed sharing the same bed) and *Gail Goes to Gay Lib.*

GAY LIBERATION

The gay liberation movement has, in recent years, grown increasingly aggressive. No longer content with demanding (rightly) that homosexuals be protected from the physical assaults of gay-bashing hetereosexuals, it now insists that everyone must accept homosexuality as normal. With a sympathetic administration in the White House for the first time in history, we can expect the movement to press for still more gains. At such a time it is important that we re-examine our attitudes towards homosexuality, in order to be able to take a clear stand in the years to come.

THE BIBLE

In the first place we must make it very clear that, in spite of all the theological head-standing on the part of liberal revisionists, the Bible plainly tells us that homosexual acts are sinful. Leviticus states unambiguously, "You shall not lie with a man as with a woman; it is an abomination" (Leviticus 18:22). Those who would claim that this passage does not apply to us, since we "live under grace, not law" must explain why we should not also be willing to accept incest, adultery, bestiality, and human sacrifice as well, since all of these are condemned in the very same passage of Leviticus. Furthermore, this prohibition is reinforced in the New Testament, where Paul writes, "Their women have exchanged natural intercourse for unnatural, and their men in turn, giving up natural relations with women, burn with lust for one another; males behave indecently with males and are paid in their own persons the fitting wage of such perversion" (Romans 1:26-28). The consummate sophistry by which the revisionists seek to obscure the all too plain meaning of this text only confirms the judgment which the Holy Spirit, through Paul, has already pronounced on them: "Claiming to be wise, they became fools..." (Romans 1:22).

UNNATURAL BEHAVIOR

Homosexuality is not only a violation of the law of God, but as Paul states, it is also unnatural. This does not mean that it does not feel natural to the practicing homosexual.. Any habitual practice, whether wholesome or harmful, will come to feel natural to its practitioner, and the attempt to discontinue the practice will feel decidedly unnatural (ask any cigarette smoker!). By unnatural we simply mean behavior which is contrary to the intent of nature. A simple understanding of human reproduction and anatomy is enough to make it clear that homosexual intercourse is unnatural. The fact that homosexual activity is often accompanied by a host of strange infectious diseases also supports this conclusion. I am not referring only to AIDS, though this is obviously the most serious of such diseases. Long before AIDS emerged on the scene, the homosexual community was afflicted with Gay Bowel Syndrome, hepatitis, and an inordinately high incidence of syphilis and gonorrhea, to name just a few. In fact, a whole literature exists dealing with the health problems unique to the homosexual community.

GAY AGENDA

With this understanding of homosexuality, we have no choice but to resist uncompromisingly the agenda of the gay rights movement, which seeks to redefine homosexuality as an "alternative lifestyle". Certainly we cannot condone physical attacks on homosexuals, or any abridgement of the normal civil rights that all enjoy. But we must condemn moves to legalize homosexual "marriages", efforts to compel religious groups to accept unrepentant homosexuals as members (or even as ministers), and attempts to subvert the minds of our children by means of curricula that portray homosexual activity as normal.

Nevertheless, while our attitude towards gay liberation can only be one of unremitting opposition, our attitude towards the individual homosexual must be no different than towards any other sinful person. For while homosexual acts are sinful, they are certainly not unforgivably sinful, nor even necessarily more sinful than many an act of which we ourselves have been guilty. The Bible has a great deal more to say about avarice, covetousness, unforgiveness, and, yes, self-righteous Phariseeism than about homosexuality. We, no less than the homosexual, stand condemned if we imagine that we are anything apart from Christ. But the good news — the news that Christ came to proclaim — is that no sin is so terrible that it cannot be forgiven, and that real healing from sin is possible through repentance and through calling on the power of the Holy Spirit. This proclamation must also be our message to the practicing homosexual: "You are in sin, and this sin is unto death — but your sin can be forgiven, and you too may enter the life of God's kingdom."

A BROTHER

But our actions must also be conformed to our proclamation. We must stand ready to accept the repentant homosexual into our fellowship and embrace him as a brother. We must stand together with him in patience and love as he struggles to win victory over his sin. For while we can never condone a slipping back into the old behavior, neither can we be more exacting of a brother tempted by homosexual urges than we are of our own selves. If our temptations were counted as sin even while we resist them, which of us could stand? If we were forever barred from fellowship after one instance of backsliding, would any of us still be in the church? As Christians we must be ready to support our homosexually-tempted brothers and sisters in their struggles, bearing and forebearing, and never ceasing to pray for the ultimate victory and liberation.

FREEDOM IS POSSIBLE

Indeed, the worst evil of the gay liberation movement is that it

61

deprives homosexuals of any possibility of victory and freedom by persuading them that the sinful way of life in which they are imprisoned is freedom, and that to accept this sinful condition as permanent and even good is victory. Truly this is a falsehood worthy of the Father of Lies.

For despite the propaganda of the gay activists, true freedom is possible. Thousands of ex-homosexuals can attest to this fact. No one can pretend that victory is easy. It may not be. One person may indeed be granted instantaneous healing from all homosexual inclinations, but many more will have to struggle with temptations for many years, and some will only find complete freedom in the life to come. Yet is it any different for the rest of us? There cannot be many Christians who have not longed and prayed, seemingly without result, for deliverance from some besetting sin. But we can never doubt that ultimately Christ will free us.

11 HOMOSEXUALITY AND RELIGION

HOMOSEXUALITY AND THE BIBLE: THE COUNTERPOINT

Duke Robinson

Duke Robinson has served as Pastor of Montclair Presbyterian church, Oakland, California, for over 25 years. Duke describes himself as "a self-affirming, unrepentant (apparently incurable) heterosexual male". Duke wrote the following article for Sequoia, *a publication of religion and public affairs. It is published by the Northern California Ecumenical Council which is located at 942 Market Street, Room 702, San Francisco, California 94102.*

Points to Consider:

1. Who are the "invisible" homosexuals serving the church?

2. How has the church led the world in hating homosexuals?

3. How do attitudes about their own sexuality influence heterosexual church people to judge homosexual people?

4. How might "conversion" of homosexuals differ from conversion of non-Christians?

Duke Robinson, "Let the Truth Be Known," **Sequoia**, July, August, 1992. Reprinted with permission. The address for **Sequoia** is 942 Market Street, San Francisco, CA 94115.

You shall know the truth and the truth shall set you free.

Jesus according to John

Homosexuality disturbs most Christian churches. They see homosexual acts — even in loving, committed relationships — as sin; they will not ordain self-affirming, sexually active gays and lesbians to the ministry or priesthood. Homosexuals do not, therefore, feel affirmed by the church. And, thus, many of them leave it or hide in the "closet" of heterosexuality.

Everyone in the church knows that these statements are true, and most would agree that we who are the church need to acknowledge them openly. At the same time, we are content to leave other important truths about homosexuals and the church unacknowledged, more hidden, unknown inside the church and out.

We thereby hurt not only others, but ourselves. We forfeit the freedom and integrity that are gained by obeying the truth and by being its agents as followers of the Christ. In truth, we who are the church suffer the negative, damaging consequences of ignorance, denial and prejudice.

If we don't want to suffer these destructive consequences, if we value our freedom and integrity as the church, if we want to be healthy spiritually, we must change our relation to these truths. We must not let them remain hidden. Indeed, we must let them be known.

Let the truth be known that many homosexuals, either raised in the church or drawn to it, remain in it, making up a mostly invisible but significant minority in the church. More than being our parents, our sons and daughters, our siblings and our friends, homosexuals are our sisters and brothers "in Christ", even though we don't see them for who they are.

Let the truth be known that many "invisible" homosexuals serve all kinds of churches as church school teachers, youth group advisors, deacons, elders, pastors, priests, evangelists and executives. Not knowing them as gays and lesbians we have welcomed and honored their evident Christian commitment and enriching contributions.

Let the truth be known that most church heterosexuals are uninformed about homosexuality. They do not study the subject; they

64

WOUNDED AND DIVIDED

Many of us grew up in the church and experienced it as a place of nurture, healing, and redemption — until we realized our gay identities. At that point we faced two primary choices: remain closeted and increasingly experience the world through a split existence, or come out and face hostility and expulsion from the church. Either path left us wounded and divided, with no community in which to integrate two fundamental parts of our identity, being gay and being Christian.

Dan Spencer, "Church at the Margins," **Christianity and Crisis**, May 25, 1992

do not know, nor do they want to know, homosexuals as persons. Thus, in ignorance, they judge all homosexuals by the behavior of a few who act out in socially offensive ways. And in prejudice they despise homosexuals who dare to feel good about themselves. Indeed, heterosexism and homophobia — the irrational fear and hatred of homosexuals — starve and stain the soul of the church.

Let the truth be known, indeed, that in the name of Christ the church has led the world in hating homosexuals, teaching hetereosexuals outside the church to condemn what they do not understand, to stereotype negatively what they fear, to see themselves as good and to judge as evil those who are different.

Let the truth be known that church heterosexuals tend to make two arrogant judgments against homosexuals:

1) that homosexuals choose their sexual orientation in sinful defiance of God — all the while admitting that we did not "choose" our own heterosexuality; and 2) that homosexuality is an arrested development, a deviation resulting from psychosocial damage, an aberration — all without support from scholarly biblical study or from the research of behavioral scientists.

Let the truth be known clearly that the claim of church homophobics that they "hate the sin and love the sinner" does not wash with thinking persons in general and with homosexuals in particular, especially those who have been victims of the ridicule, discrimination, and violence nurtured by heterosexual prejudice and bigotry.

Let the truth be known that most devout, heterosexual church people are surprised, confused and overpowered by their own sexuality — which they tend to see as dirty, as sin; that to talk about sexual matters makes them uncomfortable; and that while they regularly feel guilty about and confess to God their sexual thoughts and feelings and acts as sin, they ignore and refuse to confess as sin their hatred and demeaning treatment of homosexuals.

Let the truth be known that most church heterosexuals condone the use of a wooden biblical literalism and "prooftexts" to support a case against homosexuality. They appeal to a handful of questionable Bible verses, and to their own personal aversions to homosexuality, rather than to Jesus' gospel of unconditional love and ethic of respect for everyone.

Let the truth be known that church people who try to convert or to "cure" lesbians and gays do not work to change them into women and men who are more loving of God and neighbor, persons who will bear the burdens of people who suffer, those who will work for a just society and a cleaner environment, but simply into heterosexuals. And thus, they confuse homosexuals and others as to the nature and the purpose of the gospel.

Let the truth be known that most of our churches will gladly ordain gay and lesbian applicants who will lie about their sexual orientation, or who will promise never to engage in sexual acts; and that our churches thereby, in the name of Christ, ask homosexuals not for responsible freedom, for honesty, and for self-esteem, but for a life of repression, deception and self-hatred.

Let the truth be known, too, that the Protestants who have made much of their denominations' official statements against ordaining sexually active, self-affirming homosexuals, have generally done absolutely nothing in response to equally strong denominational directives to fight homophobia in their churches.

And finally, **let the truth be known** that the gracious, forebearing refusal of homosexuals "to return evil for evil" stands in stark and illuminating contrast to how the church's heterosexual majority has degraded them; and that their Christlike forgiveness of heterosexuals calls the homophobic Church to accept that forgiveness and to stop abusing homosexuals.

The First Century church asserts through Jesus' lips that the truth will set us free. And, indeed, over the years, truth has many times liberated the Church from the denial, ignorance, and hypocrisy that have hurt others and itself. And now the truths noted here can do that for us today.

In spite of the Church's longtime discomfort with sexuality and its entrenched animosity toward gays and lesbians, these truths can transform the homophobic church. They can throw a relentless light on our hypocrisy. They can challenge us to embrace God's unconditional love for everyone. They can lead us humbly to accept the forgiveness of lesbians and gays, and of God. And as a result, we will be free to affirm both our own sexuality and homosexuality; we will be liberated from abusing homosexuals; we will be empowered to call the world to respect the dignity of all human beings.

But if these truths remain hidden, the church will continue to demean many of its members and to suffer from ignorance and a self-righteous judgmentalism. If they are to redeem and transform with power, the church must hear and see them.

Who must spread such truths across the church? Everyone who cares about the church. Every church person who reads these words. Let the truth be known. And then keep your eyes open. Be alert. Watch. For when you see the church begin to come to terms with such truths as these, your redemption draws nigh.

WHAT IS EDITORIAL BIAS?

This activity may be used as an individualized study guide for students in libraries and resource centers or as a discussion catalyst in small group and classroom discussions.

The capacity to recognize an author's point of view is an essential reading skill. The skill to read with insight and understanding involves the ability to detect different kinds of opinions or bias. **Sex bias, race bias, ethnocentric bias, political bias,** and **religious bias** are five basic kinds of opinions expressed in editorials and all literature that attempts to persuade. They are briefly defined below.

FIVE KINDS OF EDITORIAL OPINION OR BIAS

Sex Bias — The expression of dislike for and/or feeling of superiority over the opposite sex or a particular sexual minority

Race Bias — The expression of dislike for and/or feeling of superiority over a racial group

Ethnocentric Bias — The expression of a belief that one's own group, race, religion, culture, or nation is superior. Ethnocentric persons judge others by their own standards and values.

Political Bias — The expression of political opinions and attitudes about domestic or foreign affairs

Religious Bias — The expression of a religious belief or attitude

---

Guidelines

1. From the readings in Chapter Two, locate five sentences that provide examples of editorial opinion or bias.

2. Write down each of the above sentences and determine what kind of bias each sentence represents. Is it **sex bias, race bias,**

ethnocentric bias, political bias or **religious bias?**

3. Make up one-sentence statements that would be an example of each of the following: **sex bias, race bias, ethnocentric bias, political bias** and **religious bias.**

4. See if you can locate five sentences that are **factual** statements from the readings in Chapter Two.

CHAPTER 3

HOMOSEXUALS AND THE MILITARY

12   HOMOSEXUALS AND THE MILITARY

HOMOSEXUALS IN THE MILITARY: HISTORICAL OVERVIEW

David F. Burrelli

David F. Burrelli is a defense analyst in the Foreign Affairs and National Defense Division of the Congressional Research Service (CRS), Library of Congress.

Points to Consider:

1. Prior to 1970, upon what model were the policies concerning homosexuality based?

2. How might the pre-Clinton policies be seen as a violation of civil rights?

3. What do proponents of the pre-Clinton military policy maintain?

4. Discuss: "Homosexual orientation alone should not be grounds for dismissal."

David F. Burrelli, "Homosexuals and U.S. Military Personnel Policy," **CRS Report for Congress**, January 14, 1993.

"To what extent, if any, would open homosexuality be disruptive to morale, cohesion and readiness in the ranks?"

Prior to World War I, U.S. military law did not address homosexuality. Although commanders had great discretion in the control and disciplining of their troops, specific laws, regulations or policies addressing homosexuality did not exist. The Articles of War of 1916 (effective March 1, 1917) restricted consideration of sodomy to cases of assault with the "intent to commit" sodomy. In 1951, the Uniform Code of Military Justice introduced Article 125 specifically banning sodomy (between members of the same or opposite sex) itself. Cases of assault with the intent to commit sodomy were charged under Article 134, or the General Article.

Despite a lack of laws specifically addressing the issue, numerous policies and regulations allowed for differential treatment of homosexuals or those who manifested homosexual behaviors. Prior to World War II, homosexuals were admitted into the services and, in the case of those who evidenced cross-gender mannerisms, often assigned tasks deemed relevant to the individuals' behavior and lifestyle. ("Effeminate" men were assigned away from the combat arms, for example, and placed in jobs not considered to require particularly masculine qualities, such as clerk, hospital corpsman, chaplain's assistant or camouflage specialties.)

During World War II, psychiatrists, who at the time tended to view homosexuality as a mental illness, attempted to identify and "treat" homosexuals in uniform. Numerous efforts to identify and treat homosexuals had mixed results. Failure to respond to treatment often resulted in a Section VIII discharge ("inaptness or undesirable habits"). With the social taboo against homosexuality (resulting in its concealment), the relative flexibility of personnel regulations, the need for personnel during wartime, and the inability of psychiatrists to determine who was homosexual (especially in an era of rushed wartime medical entrance examinations), meant that an undetermined number of homosexuals passed through the services without difficulty.

The policies concerning homosexuality shifted gradually from the 1940s to the 1970s. Early policies were based on a treatment and retention model. Later policies continued to accept treatment but moved increasingly toward separation (and in certain cases, punishment) of known homosexuals. Flexibility was maintained to the

Cartoon by Jeff Stahler. Reprinted with permission.

extent that certain homosexuals could be retained in situations involving "heroic service". Nevertheless, until the mid-1970s, efforts to address the issue remained under a medical model of illness, treatment, and integration into or, later, exclusion/separation from the services. . .

Department of Defense policies concerning homosexuals in military service have recently been the subject of increasing scrutiny and debate. In the 1992 presidential campaign, candidate Clinton indicated that as President he would rescind or modify the military policy excluding homosexuals from military service while maintaining strict limits on the behavior of those who serve. . .

Advocates for removing the policy view it as a violation of civil rights and fair treatment. They contend that it is unfair to separate individuals from the armed services merely as a result of their "sexual orientation". Proponents of the policy cite the need to maintain cohesion, discipline and morale within the working and living conditions imposed as a result of military service. They contend that allowing homosexuals into the service would prove disruptive to unit cohesion and, ultimately, to military readiness.

While an undetermined number of homosexuals have served in the military, such service has been performed without an open acknowledgement of their homosexuality. The question confronting policy makers remains, "To what extent, if any, would open homosexuality be disruptive to morale, cohesion and readiness in the ranks, and to what extent does any disruption justify discrimination?" Many military leaders, familiar with the military society and its rules, believe that the presence of open homosexuality would prove sufficiently disruptive to justify continuing the policy. Homosexual rights advocates, many of whom have also served in the military, believe that not only will disruptions be minimal but that the overall effectiveness and readiness of the force will improve by allowing homosexuals to serve.

Advocates for repealing the policy have generally held that restrictions should be maintained on behavior but that a homosexual "orientation" alone should not be grounds for dismissal. Distinctions between orientation and behavior, seemingly clear in the abstract, may prove difficult to make in the complex realities of everyday life.

13 HOMOSEXUALS AND THE MILITARY

ENDING DISCRIMINATION AGAINST GAYS

Senator John Kerry

John Kerry prepared the following statement for the Senate Armed Services Committee while serving as a Democratic Senator from Massachusetts.

Points to Consider:

1. How might the acceptance of gays into the military be likened to acceptance of blacks and women in the past?

2. Summarize fears about including homosexual men and women in the military.

3. How might AIDS be viewed as a reason to exclude homosexuals from the military?

4. Discuss: "Conduct — not identity — would determine eligibility for military service."

Excerpted from testimony by Senator John Kerry before the U.S. Senate Armed Services Committee, May 7, 1993.

It is a policy of intolerance that diminishes and dishonors us.

I believe it is fundamentally wrong to continue to deny to gay and lesbian Americans the right to participate in the armed forces of the United States.

Clearly, there is nothing inherent in homosexuality that makes gay Americans incapable of serving. We will never know — nor should we care — exactly how many of the 58,000 Americans listed on that black granite wall a few miles from here were gay. We will never know how many of those who lie today beneath the white crosses at Arlington were gay. We do not know how many gays and lesbians are serving in armed forces at this minute, perhaps preparing for duty in the Balkans, and how many of them may one day come home in a box.

Nor, even if the policy on gays is changed, should we bother to keep count. For no one should enter military service as a hyphenated-American, as a representative of a group of Americans, rather than as a defender of all Americans. But neither should any American who does join the military be forced to deny a fundamental part of his or her identity. We must ask how our armed forces can protect freedom if their own policies deny freedom to a significant minority of our citizens?

We must ask what we gain by continuing to codify the lie that there are not gays in the military, and by treating gay and lesbian servicepeople as second class citizens, driving them to deceit and forcing them into lives of secrecy and needless, senseless fear.

INTOLERANCE

It is a policy of intolerance that diminishes and dishonors us.

President Clinton is right to propose change, and he deserves credit — not the kind of snide sniping he has received — for asking us as a country to confront this issue now. Lifting the ban is simply one of the things we must do if we are to become a more just and honorable society. . .

For whatever reason or combination of biological, cultural and sociological circumstances, homosexuality is part of human society. We can try to deny that, but we cannot change it; and fairness to those who happen to be gay dictates instead that we concentrate on trying to understand and accept it. Most public opinion surveys

76

over the past decade indicate that this last attitude is shared by more and more Americans. And it is partly for this reason that I believe the armed forces will find it a lot easier to adjust to a new policy than many now fear.

Remember that back in the 1940s, top military officers, enlisted men and many politicians predicted disaster for the armed forces if equal treatment were accorded to black Americans. Gen. Omar Bradley said that "integration might seriously affect morale and thus affect battle efficiency." A Navy study warned of "a lowering of contentment, teamwork and discipline in the service." Senator Richard Russell warned of health risks associated with admitting African-Americans to the military, because they had a higher rate of venereal disease.

Not surprisingly, polls showed that a vast majority of white American servicemen opposed full integration before it happened. But within three years, opposition had dropped to 44% and today the idea of a segregated military is absurd. This same pattern of exaggerated fears followed by relatively smooth acceptance was repeated with the introduction of the all volunteer army and the expanding role of women. It may prove even easier with gays, because they're already there. The difference under a new policy will not be the reality — only honesty about that reality...

FEAR AND HOMOSEXUALITY

I also think a lot of the fears about openly homosexual men and women are based not on reality or personal experience, but rather on ignorance and adherence to stereotypes. The experience in foreign militaries, in police and fire departments, and in day to day life simply does not support the notion that the presence of gays and lesbians is inherently disruptive or destructive. No question, there are some gays who would make any of us uncomfortable, but these are the types of individuals who are least likely to join the military and neither homosexuals nor heterosexuals should be judged by the obnoxious few. . .

HUMAN DIFFERENCES

The fact is that military life already requires people to put aside — not deny, but put aside — differences of culture, race, religion, ideology and gender in order to perform as professionals. At least in theory, the fact that a soldier might be of Serb or Croatian or Bosnian Muslim descent could well affect their attitude towards military involvement in Bosnia and yet we would never suggest that such soldiers be screened out of the units being prepared for possible involvement in that theater. Instead, we give them the benefit of the doubt and judge them as they deserve to be judged — on behavior not status...

Lifting the ban would not give anyone license to act in a way that is unprofessional or disruptive. Sexual misconduct, harassment, inappropriate fraternization or other disruptive behavior — whether heterosexual or homosexual — would not be tolerated. All rules would be enforced, and those who violate them would be punished. Standards of military discipline would remain; only the double standards would go. Conduct — not identity — would determine eligibility for military service.

Now, what about health care costs and AIDS? This is a reasonable concern, but there are good answers to it. No one who is HIV positive is allowed in the military and all military personnel are tested regularly. If the standard is that homosexual men should be rejected because they pose an above average risk of contracting a deadly disease, my response is why stop there? Let's ban smokers.

HONORABLE SERVICE

After more than 50 years in the military and politics, I am still amazed to see how upset people can get over nothing. Lifting the ban on gays in the military isn't exactly nothing, but it's pretty damned close.

Everyone knows that gays have served honorably in the military since at least the time of Julius Caesar. They'll still be serving long after we're all dead and buried. That should not surprise anyone.

Barry M. Goldwater, "The Military Ban on Gays Is Just Plain Un-American," **Washington Post**, June 13, 1993

And let's totally eliminate the threat of AIDS by going to an all Lesbian Army.

CONCLUSION

Many of the 11,000 men and women cashiered from the military over the past decade for being gay have long since proven their value to service and country. Many won medals for bravery; many were well-regarded officers; some were highly-skilled pilots. No one has been able to make the case that they are, as a group, less courageous, less loyal, less patriotic, less talented or less worthy to serve our nation. Discharging them has cost our nation tens of millions of dollars and resulted in an immense waste of human resources and talent.

Perhaps it is true that allowing gays to serve openly will cause some disruption. It will certainly create new demands on the military and political leadership of our country to deal seriously with an issue we have avoided for too long. It may be that compromises will have to be made in order to guarantee the cohesion of particular units in particular, highly pressurized situations. But that does not justify a failure to move ahead and end the blatant discrimination that now exists. We cannot allow ourselves to be governed or controlled by the least common denominator of social attitudes.

14   HOMOSEXUALS AND THE MILITARY

MILITARY SERVICE IS NOT A CIVIL RIGHT

David Hackworth

David Hackworth, a contributing editor for defense at Newsweek, *rose from private to colonel in the U.S. Army, has eight Purple Hearts and is the most decorated living American veteran. Hackworth wrote this article for* The Washington Post.

Points to Consider:

1. What types of "morale-busting" behavior could occur with gay officers, according to Hackworth?

2. How does Hackworth justify putting aside civilian standards of equality in times of battle?

3. Why don't the "top brass" speak about gays in the military?

4. How does Hackworth characterize those who are pushing for the homosexual ban to be lifted?

David Hackworth, "Good Reasons to Keep Gays Out of the Military," **The Washington Post**, July 1992. Reprinted with permission.

Discriminations are necessary when a larger public purpose is being served.

Rep. Pat Schroeder of Colorado wanted to give women "equality and opportunity" by making them rucksack-toting grunts. Now she aims at putting homosexuals in the foxholes to "end the final bastion of discrimination." I cannot think of a better way to destroy fighting spirit and gut U.S. combat effectiveness. My credentials for saying this are over four decades of experience as a soldier or military reporter.

Despite the ban on service by homosexuals, gays have long served in the armed forces, some with distinction. Many perhaps felt no sexual inclination toward their heterosexual fellow soldiers. If they did, they had their buddies' attitudes and the Uniform Code of Military Justice hanging over their heads.

BEHAVIOR

Still, I have seen countless examples of inappropriate and morale-busting behavior.

In Italy, for example, in the postwar occupation, a gay soldier could not keep his hands off other soldiers in my squad. He disrupted discipline, mangled trust among squad members and zeroed out morale. In the same unit, the personnel major was gay. He had affairs with ambitious teenage soldiers in exchange for kicking up their test scores. This corrupted the command's promotion system and led to the commissioning of William Calley-like lieutenants not fit to lead combat soldiers.

During my second tour in the Korean War, a gay commanding officer gave combat awards to his lovers who had never been on the line. In Vietnam, a young captain in my unit was asked by the commander to go to bed with him. This almost destroyed the esprit of a fine parachute unit.

These are not isolated incidents: during my Army career I saw countless officers and NCOs who couldn't stop themselves from hitting on soldiers. The absoluteness of their authority, the lack of privacy, enforced intimacy and a 24-hour duty day made sexual urges difficult to control. The objects of their affection were impressionable lads who, searching for a caring role model, sometimes ended up in a gay relationship they might not have sought.

Cartoon by Richard Wright. Reprinted with permission.

POPULAR ATTITUDES

A majority of American citizens, according to polls, support Schroeder's bill. Many people look at the armed forces as they do the post office, the Bank of America or General Motors — an 8-to-5 institution where discrimination on the basis of sexual orientation is against basic freedom, human rights and the American way of life.

If these polls are true, a lot of people don't understand what war is about. Sure, banning gays from defending their country is discriminatory. But discriminations are necessary when a larger public purpose is being served. Civilian standards of fairness and equality don't apply down where the body bags are filled.

On the battlefield, what allows men to survive is combat units made up of disciplined team players, who are realistically trained and led by caring skippers who set the example and know their trade. When all of these factors are in sync, a unit has the right stuff. It becomes tight, a family, and clicks like a professional football team. Spirited men who place their lives in their buddie's hands are the most essential element in warfare. The members of such combat teams trust one another totally.

SEX AND SERVICE MEMBERS

One doesn't need to be a field marshal to understand that sex between service members undermines those critical factors that produce discipline, military orders, spirit and combat effectiveness. Mix boys and girls, gays and straight in close quarters such as the barracks or the battlefield, and both sexual contact and the consequent breakdown of morale are inevitable.

Many bright people are pushing for the ban to be lifted. I suspect that few if any have been down in the trenches, but I have no doubt their psychological-sociological-political clout will have considerable influence even if they don't have a clue what combat is about.

Unfortunately, most of the top brass won't sound off. They duck and weave and offer hollow and spurious Pentagonese double-talk reasons for continuing the ban — reasons that only fuel the pro-gay argument. But they have told me in the "G" ring of the Pentagon that they're "against it, but sounding off would be the kiss of death, like opposing women in combat — a career killer, you know."

PROS AND WARRIORS

I hope that our lawmakers will visit Quantico and Fort Benning before they vote, and ask Marine gunnery sergeants and Army platoon sergeants what a few gays would do to the fighting spirit of units. These pros told me: gays are not wanted by straight men or women in their showers, toilets, foxholes or fighting units. They say that in combat young men face death constantly, and what allows them to make it through the hell of it all is a feeling of toughness, invincibility and total trust in their buddies.

My experience with warriors in over eight years of roaming the killing fields in seven wars confirms what these old salts are saying. A serving lieutenant general recently wrote to me, "Ask Pat

Schroeder if she'd like her kids under a gay first sergeant who might use his rank and authority to demand sexual favors from his subordinate 18-year-old kids. We just had that occur in my command."

MORALE

No doubt advocates of gays in combat units will argue that they don't approve of demanding sexual favors and that the first sergeant deserved what he got — a court-martial. The problem is, all the court-martials and regulations in the world can't prevent the kind of morale problems that a change in the law is bound to create. Sure, the first sergeant is serving hard time at Fort Leavenworth, but Pat Schroeder and the two dozen lawmakers who support her bill must also ask themselves what happened to the morale and fighting spirit of his unit.

15   HOMOSEXUALS AND THE MILITARY

A NEW POLICY ON HOMOSEXUALS: THE POINT

President Bill Clinton

President Clinton prepared the following remarks for the National Defense University at Fort McNair, Washington, D.C.

Points to Consider:

1. Summarize the fears of military people opposed to lifting the ban on homosexuals.

2. How is possible misconduct by homosexuals in the military covered?

3. Explain: "Servicemen and women will be judged by their conduct, not their sexual orientation."

4. What parallel might be drawn between including homosexuals in our police and fire departments?

Excerpted from a speech by President Bill Clinton at the National Defense University, Fort McNair, Washington, D.C., July 19, 1993.

There have been and are homosexuals in the military service who serve with distinction.

I have come here today to discuss a difficult challenge and one which has received an enormous amount of publicity and public and private debate over the last several months — our nation's policy toward homosexuals in the military. I believe the policy I am announcing today represents a real step forward...

THE GULF WAR

Let me review the events which bring us here today. Before I ran for President, this issue was already upon us. Some of the members of the military returning from the Gulf War announced their homosexuality in order to protest the ban. The military's policy has been questioned in college ROTC programs. Legal challenges have been filed in court, including one that has since succeeded. In 1991, Secretary of Defense Dick Cheney was asked about reports that the Defense Department spent an alleged $500 million to separate and replace about 17,000 homosexuals from the military service during the 1980s, in spite of the findings of a government report saying there was no reason to believe that they could not serve effectively and with distinction...

CENTRAL FACTS

The central facts of this issue are not much in dispute. First, notwithstanding the ban, there have been and are homosexuals in the military service who serve with distinction. I have had the privilege of meeting some of these men and women, and I have been deeply impressed by their devotion to duty and to country.

Second, there is no study showing them to be less capable or more prone to misconduct than heterosexual soldiers. Indeed, all the information we have indicates that they are not less capable or more prone to misbehavior.

Third, misconduct is already covered by the laws and rules which also cover activities that are improper by heterosexual members of the military.

Fourth, the ban has been lifted in other nations and in police and fire departments in our country with no discernible negative impact on unit cohesion or capacity to do the job, though there is, admittedly, no absolute analogy to the situation we face and no study

Cartoon by Steve Sack. Reprinted by permission of the **Star Tribune**, Minneapolis.

bearing on this specific issue.

Fifth, even if the ban were lifted entirely, the experience of other nations and police and fire departments in the United States indicates that most homosexuals would probably not declare their sexual orientation openly, thereby making an already hard life even more difficult in some circumstances. . .

Clearly, the American people are deeply divided on this issue, with most military people opposed to lifting the ban because of the feared impact on unit cohesion, rooted in disapproval of homosexual lifestyles, and the fear of invasion of privacy of heterosexual soldiers who must live and work in close quarters with homosexual military people.

However, those who have studied this issue extensively have discovered an interesting fact. People in this country who are aware of having known homosexuals are far more likely to support lifting the ban. In other words, they are likely to see this issue in terms of individual conduct and individual capacity instead of the claims of a group with which they do not agree; and also to be able to imagine how this ban could be lifted without a destructive impact on group cohesion and morale.

THE COMPROMISE

Shortly after I took office and reaffirmed my position, the foes of lifting the ban in the Congress moved to enshrine the ban in law. I asked that congressional action be delayed for six months while the Secretary of Defense worked with the Joint Chiefs to come up with a proposal for changing our current policy. I then met with the Joint Chiefs to hear their concerns and asked them to try to work through the issue with Secretary Aspin. I wanted to handle the matter in this way on grounds of both principle and practicality. . .

During this time many dedicated Americans have come forward to state their own views on this issue. Most, but not all, of the military testimony has been against lifting the ban. But support for changing the policy has come from distinguished combat veterans including Senators Bob Kerrey, Chuck Robb, and John Kerry in the United States Congress. It has come from Lawrence Korb, who enforced the gay ban during the Reagan administration; and from former Senator Barry Goldwater, a distinguished veteran, former Chairman of the Senate Arms Services Committee, founder of the Arizona National Guard, and patron saint of the conservative wing of the Republican Party.

Senator Goldwater's statement, published in *The Washington Post* recently, made it crystal clear that when this matter is viewed as an issue of individual opportunity and responsibility rather than one of alleged group rights, this is not a call for cultural license, but rather a reaffirmation of the American value of extending opportunity to responsible individuals and of limiting the role of government over citizens' private lives.

On the other hand, those who oppose lifting the ban are clearly focused not on the conduct of individual gay service members, but on how non-gay service members feel about gays in general and, in particular, those in the military service.

A NEW POLICY

These past few days I have been in contact with the Secretary of Defense as he has worked through the final stages of this policy with the Joint Chiefs. We now have a policy that is a substantial advance

88

over the one in place when I took office. I have ordered Secretary Aspin to issue a directive consisting of these essential elements:

One, servicemen and women will be judged based on their conduct, not their sexual orientation.

Two, therefore, the practice, now six months old, of not asking about sexual orientation in the enlistment procedure will continue.

Three, an open statement by a service member that he or she is a homosexual will create a rebuttable presumption that he or she intends to engage in prohibited conduct, but the service member will be given an opportunity to refute that presumption; in other words, to demonstrate that he or she intends to live by the rules of conduct that apply in the military service.

And four, all provisions of the Uniform Code of Military Justice will be enforced in an even-handed manner as regards both heterosexuals and homosexuals. And, thanks to the policy provisions agreed on by the Joint Chiefs, there will be a decent regard to the legitimate privacy and associational rights of all service members.

Just as is the case under current policy, unacceptable conduct, either heterosexual or homosexual, will be unacceptable 24 hours a day, seven days a week, from the time a recruit joins the service until the day he or she is discharged. Now, as in the past, every member of our military will be required to comply with the Uniform Code of Military Justice, which is federal law and military regulations, at all times and in all places. . .

Our military is a conservative institution, and I saw that in the very best sense, for its purpose is to conserve the fighting spirit of our troops; to conserve the resources and the capacity of our troops; to conserve the military lessons acquired during our nation's existence; to conserve our very security; and yes, to conserve the liberties of the American people. Because it is a conservative institution, it is right for the military to be wary of sudden changes. Because it is an institution that embodies the best of America and must reflect the society in which it operates, it is also right for the military to make changes when the time for change is at hand.

I strongly believe that our military, like our society, needs the talents of every person who wants to make a contribution and who is ready to live by the rules. That is the heart of the policy that I have announced today. I hope in your heart you will find the will and the desire to support it and to lead our military in incorporating it into our nation's great asset and the world's best fighting force.

16 HOMOSEXUALS AND THE MILITARY

A NEW POLICY ON HOMOSEXUALS: THE COUNTERPOINT

Molly Ivins & *Human Events*

Molly Ivins is a nationally syndicated columnist and television com-mentator. Human Events *is a national magazine of political and social opinion.*

Points to Consider:

1. Rather than "homosexuality is incompatible with military ser-vice," what might the policy better say?

2. How is the gay movement likened to the black movement of the 1960's?

3. Why is the gay community dissatisfied with President Clinton's new policy?

4. How realistic is the threat of increased AIDS cases under the new policy?

Molly Ivins, "Compromise Criminalizes Words More Than Deeds," **Star Tribune**, Minneapolis, July 22, 1993. By permission of Molly Ivins and Creators Syndicate. And "Clinton Unleashes Pro-Gay Plan," **Human Events**, July 31, 1993. Reprinted with permission.

The more sensible policy would be: "Sexual misconduct is incompatible with military service."

The best suggestion so far for a compromise on gays in the military comes from the cartoonist for the *Atlanta Constitution* who thinks we should allow gays in the military on Mondays, Wednesdays and Fridays.

THE COMPROMISE

The compromise we're getting makes about that much sense. Pointing out that it's a silly compromise has no bearing on whether or not it's the best that can be done at this point. As the late Edmund Burke pointed out, "All government — indeed, every human benefit and enjoyment, every virtue and every prudent act — is founded on compromise and barter." Take that half a loaf when you can get it.

Still. Yet. But. However. This is not an intelligent compromise, and I suspect the military will come to regret it. From the point of view of both discipline and morale, the military would be far better off with a simple policy stating that sexual misconduct of any kind, homosexual or heterosexual, from sexual harassment to sexual assault, would be grounds for punishment and/or dismissal.

TALK AND CONDUCT

The oddity of the current compromise is that it actually punishes talk more than conduct. A gay soldier can frequent gay bars or go to a gay demonstration, but talking about it would be grounds for opening an investigation. You notice the further silliness of "don't ask, don't tell, don't pursue": If by saying "I am gay" a soldier opens himself or herself to investigation, what does that have to do with whether or not said soldier has committed any sexual misconduct? If the fact of being gay alone is still grounds for dismissal of an exemplary soldier, then the injustice remains unaddressed.

This is a policy designed to keep gays in the closet. As a practical matter, it is highly unlikely that many gays in the military will come out. More reticence on the subject of sex is probably desirable in this society generally, but I doubt even the American armed forces can stop people from talking about sex.

Cartoon by Mark Cullum. Reprinted by permission of Coply News Service.

THE POLICY

The heart of the problem is the stated policy that "homosexuality is incompatible with military service." It rather patently is not, because gay soldiers have done well in the military in the past and continue to do so today. Changing the policy to "homosexual conduct is incompatible" doesn't get us much further because celibacy has never been a popular option for people of any sexual orientation. Again, the more sensible policy would be: "Sexual misconduct is incompatible with military service."

Meanwhile, the whole insanely wasteful bureaucracy we have to pay for, whose sole mission is to snoop on the private lives of military personnel, remains in place. We will apparently continue to pay photographers to break into people's bedrooms, military police to hang around gay bars and clerks to process all the forms they fill out — none of which does much to protect the nation from foreign countries.

To further complicate this unsatisfactory situation, Senator Sam Nunn has announced that he plans to propose a law regulating "homosexual acts and statements". Bob Sherrill once entitled a book of his *Military Justice Is to Justice as Military Music Is to Music.* However, the writ of the Constitution, while limited in the military, still stands. It will be an awful constitutional mess if Congress runs around trying to decide what is a permissible statement and what is not.

COMPROMISE

It may be that this silly compromise will give us all a chance to realize that nothing horrible is going to happen if we admit that there are gays in the military. Not only will nothing horrible happen, but nothing at all will happen, as the recent experience in Canada proves. No one could even get a story out of the court-ordered change there, as the only result was that nothing changed. The military went right on being the military.

The study by the Laboratory of Biochemistry of the National Cancer Institute that was published in *Science,* suggesting that homosexuality is at least partly genetically determined, will, if confirmed, probably have a long-term impact on attitudes toward gays. But I suspect it will take time. Jonathan Tolins, a gay playwright, wrote in *Newsweek* that his first reaction to the news of the study was excitement and relief.

CIVIL RIGHTS

"So much of the anti-gay legal and social argument is based on the premise that it is a learned behavior and an immoral choice. This would prove them wrong!" But Tolins said he gave up his fantasy that "Pat Robertson might look at a chart of DNA and say, "Well, I'll be; I've been wrong all this time. I'd better send an apology." His fantasy lasted about a minute and a half, which is about how long it took for anti-gay groups to attack the study.

I think it's long past time for all of us to realize that this country is undergoing another civil rights movement and that everything we learned from the great black movement of the 50s and 60s applies this time, too. That a minority denied full legal rights needs lawyers and demonstrators, people working both inside and outside the system. And that sooner or later, those of us who consider ourselves bystanders have to answer the question: "Which side are you on?"

94

The new policy will cost "billions of dollars" for the treatment of new AIDS cases.

Last week President Clinton finally announced what his new policy would be regarding openly homosexual members of the armed forces. That policy quickly became summarized as "Don't ask, don't tell, and don't pursue." Despite instant cries of "betrayal" from gay militants, conservatives were dismayed by the announcement, believing it to represent an important advance for the homosexual agenda.

Conservatives were especially disheartened by the behavior of the Joint Chiefs of Staff who beamed happily throughout Clinton's speech and, for all the world, seemed to have caved in completely to the reassuring blandishments of Administration lawyers that the new policy would be an improvement on the old and that it was time to move on to more important issues. . .

In its specifics, the new Clinton policy rejects the old practice of asking recruits about their sexual orientation, and it likewise forbids commanders from beginning an investigation based on hearsay evidence or allegations. It also permits a bewildering array of behaviors which would have justified an immediate investigation under the old policy.

For example, service members will now be permitted to go to gay bars, attend gay marches and demonstration, read gay magazines in the barracks, and even display desk photos of gay lovers — all without any concern that these behaviors might justify an inquiry from military authorities. However, service members attending a gay march while wearing tee shirts or carrying banners, either of which proclaim their pride in being homosexual, apparently will be subject to questioning.

Pentagon officials have said that an "extensive field guide" will eventually have to be published "to help commanders judge whether or not to investigate somebody." The proposed guide, they say, will turn a blind eye to a serviceman's wearing of earrings or the leather clothing associated with sado-masochism, but will draw the line at "flamboyant costumes"...

Loaded with such manifest absurdities, the Clinton changes clearly relax the impediments to homosexuals filling the ranks, with all the accompanying morale damage and escalating risks. Hence, it is more important than ever for voters to barrage Coats and his fellow senators with declarations of support for their resistance to this disrupting, damaging and dangerous new policy. Of late, we're told, conservatives who voiced objections last winter and spring have become mute, and gays have increased the volume of letters, telegrams and phone calls to political representatives.

(Some legislation restoring the pre-Clinton policy already does exist in the House — the Military Readiness Act of 1993 — where it was introduced by GOP Rep. Bob Dornan of California earlier this year. Though it has 104 co-sponsors it is not likely to be voted on, since Democrats have the parliamentary ability to block its progress.)

GAY/ACLU REACTION

Clinton had hardly finished announcing the promised policy changes before his gay critics weighed in with considerable invective. San Francisco homosexuals staged a "Darkness at Noon" rally and one of that city's supervisors, avowed lesbian Carole Migden said, "We're bitterly disappointed. We've been let down."

Yet another lesbian San Francisco city supervisor explained, "It's a cruel hoax to say he's supporting equity and making an honorable compromise when he's allowing us to be homosexual in our minds only."

One Bay Area gay demonstrator, Olivia Partridge, a lawyer who not only voted for Clinton but contributed $1,000 to his campaign and donated hundreds of hours of volunteer work, was so livid that she told reporters, "I will vote for Senator Jesse Helms before I vote for Bill Clinton. . . At least we know what Helms stands for; I will never be lied to like that again."

A sister in the movement, Lisa Dettmer of the Lesbian Avengers, warned ominously, "We won't settle for anything less than a complete lifting of the ban, and our fuse is short. Clinton doesn't want to experience the wrath of unbridled lesbian anger."

CONSERVATIVE RESPONSES

Expressing worries felt by many, Rep. Bob Dornan (R.-Calif.) predicted that the new policy will cost "billions of dollars" for the treatment of new AIDS cases, and he said he feared that the safety of the military's blood supply might be compromised.

Gary Bauer, president of the Family Research Council, made the obvious political point when he observed, "[This] undercuts the idea that Clinton is a moderate, because he still comes across as beholden to the gay rights constituency..." Elaine Donnelly, president for the Center for Military Readiness, told us that she is convinced that, given enough grass-roots support, Congress will vote to return to the policy that has served America so well over the years.

Donelly added, "Defense Secretary Aspin says the military has a 'new mission'...of dealing...with social issues...such as the way that Americans deal with sexual orientation. But this is not the mission of the military; the armed forces are there to defend the country. They should not be used for political payoffs or involuntary social experimentation. The question is not whether the President has betrayed the interests of homosexuals, but whether he should be allowed to betray the interests of the military in order to pay off a political debt."

Donnelly was especially exercised over the possibility that questions about the sexual practices of blood donors might be prohibited. "Even soldiers or sailors who donate blood at a civilian installation are asked if they have engaged in high-risk sexual behaviors," noted Donnelly, who then posed the question: "Why would you not want to know if the blood about to be given to a wounded soldier might be contaminated?"

Donnelly stressed that she had many other concerns as well. "To raise just a few," she continued, "if a junior service member strikes a senior service member who is attempting to engage in sexual contact, will he be vulnerable to the serious charges that normally apply to those striking superiors?

Will currently serving men and women be permitted to leave the armed forces honorably because the conditions of their contract have been considerably altered?

Perhaps, most importantly, since the new policy does not affirm the old standard that 'homosexuality is incompatible with military service', on what grounds can homosexuals be discharged from the service at all?"

INTERPRETING
EDITORIAL CARTOONS

This activity may be used as an individualized study guide for students in libraries and resource centers or as a discussion catalyst in small group and classroom discussions.

Although cartoons are usually humorous, the main intent of most political cartoonists is not to entertain. Cartoons express serious social comment about important issues. Using graphic and visual arts, the cartoonist expresses opinions and attitudes. By employing an entertaining and often light-hearted visual format, cartoonists may have as much or more impact on national and world issues as editorial and syndicated columnists.

Points to Consider

1. Examine the cartoon on page 93.

2. How would you describe the message of the cartoon? Try to describe the message in one to three sentences.

3. Do you agree with the message expressed in the cartoon? Why or why not?

4. Does the cartoon support the author's point of view in any of the readings in this publication? If the answer is yes, be specific about which reading or readings and why.

5. Are any of the readings in Chapter Three in basic agreement with the cartoon?

CHAPTER 4

THE GAY FAMILY

17   THE GAY FAMILY

GAY MARRIAGE AND THE COURTS: AN OVERVIEW

The Washington Post

The Hawaii Supreme Court has become the first in the country to rule that a state may not be able to prohibit gays from marrying. The decision gives gays and lesbians broad protection under the state's constitution.

The court said any state regulation that sets up limits based on sex (in this case, that men may marry only women and that women may marry only men) can be defended only if the state shows that it has "compelling" reasons. That is the toughest legal test for a state to meet and traditionally has required it to prove that public safety is at stake.

The ruling handed down marked the second time in the past year that state courts have found protection for gays in state constitutions. The Kentucky Supreme Court safeguarded privacy rights for homosexuals when it struck down an anti-sodomy law. Together, the decisions show how new legal avenues for gays have opened, at the same time that gays are winning more social acceptance and political status.

"We're thrilled, and we're planning our wedding," said Ninia Baehr, one of the parties to the Hawaii case, who has been trying for nearly three years to marry another woman.

The rulings also illustrate how activists on a range of issues often turn to state courts for vindication. Many state constitutions, as in Hawaii and Kentucky, offer broader protections for individual rights than the federal Constitution, and state high courts are the final arbiters of the rights in those documents. Further, because of the dominance of conservatives on the federal bench, some liberals believe they can make more headway in state courts.

The Hawaii ruling reinstated a lawsuit by three gay couples, two female and one male, who were denied marriage licenses under a Hawaii statute that prohibits people from marrying someone of the same sex. A lower court had dismissed their case, saying no law supported their claim. But the state Supreme Court ruled that under the state constitution's guarantee of equal protection of the laws, any sex-based classification is "suspect", putting it in a special category traditionally reserved for regulations that make distinctions based on race.

The couples said they wanted to marry for societal affirmation and for the financial and legal benefits married couples enjoy. The case now returns to a trial court for the state to try to prove it has a "compelling" reason for the law.

18 THE GAY FAMILY

A CASE FOR GAY MARRIAGE

Brent Hartinger

Brent Hartinger is a free-lance writer based in Seattle, Washington. Hartinger wrote the following article for Commonweal, *a Catholic publication of social and religious commentary, based in New York City. This article was presented as part of a debate in* Commonweal *and does not represent the magazine's point of view.*

Points to Consider:

1. Summarize the financial benefits of same-sex marriage.

2. What is the unwanted consequence of limiting gay couples to "domestic partnership"?

3. Explain: "Encouraging gay monogamy is simple rational public health policy."

4. How might gay marriage strengthen the family?

5. Why would gay marriage not necessarily endorse homosexual behavior?

Brent Hartinger, "A Case for Gay Marriage," **Commonweal**, November 22, 1991. Reprinted with permission. This article was presented as part of a debate in **Commonweal** and does not represent the magazine's point of view.

Indeed, the compelling state interest lies in permitting gay unions.

Denmark became the first industrialized country to permit same-sex unions (since then, one-fifth of all marriages performed there have been homosexual ones.) However sporadic, this represents a major victory for gay men and lesbians for whom legal marriage is not an option...

DOMESTIC PARTNERSHIPS

Legally and financially, much is at stake. Most employee benefit plans — which include health insurance, parental leave, and bereavement leave — extend only to legal spouses. Marriage also allows partners to file joint income taxes, usually saving them money. Social Security can give extra payment to qualified spouses. And assets left from one legal spouse to the other after death are not subject to estate taxes. If a couple splits up, there is the issue of visitation rights for adopted children or offspring conceived by artificial insemination. And then there are issues of jurisprudence (a legal spouse cannot be compelled to testify against his or her partner) and inheritance, tenancy, and conservatorship: pressing concerns for many gays as a result of AIDS.

In terms of numbers alone, a need exists. An estimated 10 percent of the population — about 25 million Americans — is exclusively or predominantly homosexual in sexual orientation, and upwards of 50 percent of the men and about 70 percent of the women are in long-term, committed relationships. A 1990 survey of 1,266 lesbian and gay couples found that 82 percent of the male couples and 75 percent of the female ones share all or part of their incomes.

As a result, many lesbians and gays have fought for "domestic partnership" legislation to extend some marital and family benefits to unmarried couples — cohabiting partners either unwilling or, in the case of homosexuals, unable to marry. In New York City, for example, unmarried municipal workers who have lived with their partners at least a year may register their relationships with the personnel department, attesting to a "close and committed" relationship "involving shared responsibilities," and are then entitled to bereavement leave.

But such a prescription is inadequate; the protections and benefits are only a fraction of those resulting from marriage — and are avail-

103

DECISION TO MARRY

The decision whether or not to marry belongs properly to individuals — not the government. Yet at present, all 50 states deny that choice to millions of gay and lesbian Americans. While marriage has historically required a male partner and a female partner, history alone cannot sanctify injustice. If tradition were the only measure, most states would still limit matrimony to partners of the same race.

Thomas B. Stoddard, "Gay Adults Should Not Be Denied Benefits of Marriage," **New York Times**, March, 1989

able to only a small percentage of gays in a handful of cities (in the above-mentioned survey, considerably less than 10 percent of lesbian and gay couples were eligible for any form of shared job benefits). Even the concept of "domestic partnership" is seriously flawed. What constitutes a "domestic partnership"? Could roommates qualify? A woman and her live-in maid? It could take an array of judicial decision making to find out.

Further, because the benefits of "domestic partnership" are allotted to couples without much legal responsibility — and because the advantages of domestic partnership are necessarily allowed for unmarried heterosexual partners as well as homosexual ones — domestic partnership has the unwanted consequence of weakening traditional marriage. Society has a vested interest in stable, committed relationships — especially, as in the case of most heterosexual couples, when children are concerned. But by eliminating the financial and legal advantages to marriage, domestic partnership dilutes that institution.

Society already has a measure of relational union — it's called marriage, and it's not at all difficult to ascertain: you're either married or you're not.

Yet for unmarried heterosexual couples, marriage is at least an option. Gay couples have no such choice — and society also has an interest in committed, long-lasting relationships even between homosexuals. An estimated three to five million homosexuals have parented children within heterosexual relationships, and at least 1,000 children were born to lesbian or gay couples in the San Francisco area alone in just the last five years. None of the recent thirty-five studies on homosexual parents has shown that parental sexual orientation has any adverse effect on children (and the children of gays are no more likely to be gay themselves). Surely increased stability in the relationships of lesbians and gay men could only help the gays themselves and their many millions of children...

GAY MARRIAGE

Indeed, the compelling state interest lies in permitting gay unions. In the wake of AIDS, encouraging gay monogamy is simply rational public health policy. Just as important, gay marriage would reduce the number of closeted gays who marry heterosexual partners, as an estimated 20 percent of all gays do, in an effort to conform to social pressure — but at enormous cost to themselves, their children, and their opposite-sex spouses. It would reduce the atmosphere of ridicule and abuse in which the children of homosexual parents grow up. And it would reduce the number of shameful parents who disown their children or banish their gay teen-agers to lives of crime, prostitution, and drug abuse, or to suicide (psychologists estimate that gay youth comprise up to 30 percent of all teen suicides, and one Seattle study found that a whopping 40 percent of that city's street kids may be lesbian or gay, most having run away or been expelled from intolerant homes). Gay marriage wouldn't weaken the family; it would strengthen it.

The unprecedented social legitimacy given gay partnerships — and homosexuality in general — would have other societal benefits as well: it would dramatically reduce the widespread housing and job discrimination, and verbal and physical violence experienced by most lesbians and gays, clear moral and social evils.

Of course, legal and religious gay marriage wouldn't, as some writers claim, "celebrate" or be "an endorsement" of homosexual sexual behavior — any more than heterosexual marriage celebrates heterosexual sex or endorses it; gay marriage would celebrate the loving, committed relationship between two individuals, a relationship in which sexual behavior is one small part. Still, the legalization of gay marriage, while not making homosexual sexual behavior any more prevalent, would remove much of the stigma concerning such behavior, at least that which takes place within the confines of "marriage". And if the church sanctions such unions, a further, moral legitimacy will be granted. In short, regardless of the potential societal gains, should society and the church reserve a centuries-old moral stand that condemns homosexual sexual behavior?

We have no choice; the premises upon which the moral stand are based have changed. Science now acknowledges the existence of a homosexual sexual orientation, like heterosexuality, a fundamental affectional predisposition...

CONCLUSION

Moral condemnation of homosexual sexual behavior is often founded on the belief that sex and marriage are — and should be — inexorably linked with child-rearing; because lesbians and gay men are physiologically incapable of creating children alone, all such sexual behavior is deemed immoral — and gays are considered unsuitable to the institution of marriage. But since moral sanction is not withheld from infertile couples or those who intend to remain childless, this standard is clearly being inconsistently — and unfairly — applied.

Some cite the promiscuity of some male gays as if this is an indication that all homosexuals are incapable or undeserving of marriage. But this standard is also inconsistently applied; it has never been seriously suggested that the existence of promiscuous heterosexuals invalidate all heterosexuals from the privilege of marriage. And if homosexuals are more likely than heterosexuals to be promiscuous — and if continual, harsh condemnation hasn't altered that fact — the sensible solution would seem to be to try to lure gays back to the monogamous fold by providing efforts in that direction with some measure of respect and social support; something gay marriage would definitely provide.

19 THE GAY FAMILY

DON'T LEGALIZE SAME SEX MARRIAGE

Jeffrey Hart

Jeffrey Hart is a professor of English at Dartmouth College, Hanover, New Hampshire. Hart is a prominent, conservative journalist and spokesperson.

Points to Consider:

1. Explain how homosexuals might be seen to have a legal advantage over heterosexuals.

2. According to Hart, what has been society's attitude toward homosexuals?

3. How might President Clinton's definition of "family" be seen as weakening the norm?

Jeffrey Hart, "Gay Rights Are Extra-Constitutional," **Human Events**, November 14, 1992. Reprinted with special permission of King Features Syndicate.

There is no society known to history that has regarded homosexuality as a version of the normal.

Homosexuality used to be called "the love that dare not speak its name," but today it seems to be the love that will not shut up. We are hearing insistent demands for "gay rights", and Bill Clinton has explicitly endorsed the idea. But what does the term mean?

Homosexuals, being citizens, have the same constitutional rights as all the rest of us. They have the right to vote, for example, the right to a fair trial if an offense is charged, the right to free speech and freedom of religion and assembly. Like anyone else, they can bring suit in court. And so on and so forth. They have the rights of citizens.

SPECIAL RIGHTS

But they are now demanding special rights specific to homosexuals. We have recently seen the "special rights" theme implemented in the new laws against so-called hate crimes. Assaulting a member of a victim group is now, legally, a more serious offense than assaulting...well, me. Assault and battery is normally a felony offense, but if you assault a certified victim you can get extra time in prison.

Thus certified victims have a legally privileged position. In addition, certified victims have never to my knowledge been charged with committing a "hate crime". The young black man named, oddly, Christian Prince, who killed the Yale student is never said to have acted out of hateful motives. The black and Hispanic thugs who killed Brian Watson on a New York subway platform are never said to have acted out of "hate".

And thus, equivalently, homosexuals already possess special rights. Someone who gets into an altercation with a homosexual had better be prepared to be charged with committing a hate crime. The homosexual now has a legal advantage over the non-homosexual.

GAY RIGHTS

But the demand for "gay rights" extends much further. It involves, as I understand it, the legislation of homosexual marriage. It involves the "right" of homosexual couples to adopt children, and so forth. These are revolutionary demands, in the sense that no

DOMESTIC PARTNERS

Gays (homosexual and lesbian activists) are now battling on the domestic front to achieve status as "domestic partners". This might seem innocent enough, when you reflect on the sordid nature of gay sexual practices, but it would undermine irrevocably the traditional understanding of what constitutes a marriage and a family.

Howard Hurwitz, "Are Gays Domestic Partners?" **Human Events**, March 10, 1990

society in recorded history has even dreamed of any such things. Some societies have severely persecuted homosexuals, but most have taken a tolerant live-and-let-live attitude toward this aberration, as long as it did not become too visible and intrusive.

Oscar Wilde, for example, was a popular writer and a society pet until he went too far and sued for libel. Then the full weight of the law fell upon him and he ended up behind bars. Society regards such people as Truman Capote and Gore Vidal as amusing clowns, but does not persecute them.

HOMOSEXUALITY

There is no society known to history that has regarded homosexuality as a version of the normal. All societies have regarded male-female sexuality as the norm. To accord homosexual relations a legal presumption of normality would be something new in human history, and, if only on that account, something of which to be extremely wary.

In his acceptance speech at the Democratic National Convention, Clinton defined the word "family" in a very broad way, including single mothers, single fathers and homosexual couples. By including these various forms of association in the norm designated by the word "family", Clinton was weakening the norm.

CIVILIZED NORMS

Civilization is profoundly a matter of norms, although it learns to live tacitly with aberrations as long as they do not make too much noise. The norm of the family has been defined by millennia of human experience, and it does not include the relationship between

Oscar Wilde and Lord Alfred Douglas, his catamite.

If we weaken the norms, history suggests that the norms will have their revenge. It seems to be one of the hallmarks of contemporary liberalism that it not only ignores the experience of norms but actually seeks to undermine them. Beware.

THE GAY FAMILY

GAYS AND LESBIANS ARE CHOOSING TO BE PARENTS

Ellen Uzelac

Ellen Uzelac wrote the following article in her capacity as West Coast Correspondent for The Baltimore Sun.

Points to Consider:

1. Briefly describe the gay and lesbian parenting movement.

2. About how many children in the United States have homosexual parents?

3. What are some of the psychological considerations that can make gay parenting successful?

4. Summarize research comparing children of lesbian and gay parents and children of heterosexual parents.

open
Thesis

Never before in the history of the U.S. family have so many children been raised by openly gay parents.

Joy Schulenburg will never forget the dismay she felt when, wearing her "Baby in the Oven" T-shirt, she walked into a cafe and was told: "What are you doing here? This is a dyke bar." Schulenburg was upset not that she was in a lesbian bar but that lesbians should dismiss her so curtly and so readily: Schulenburg is a lesbian herself. Schulenburg, 33, became pregnant in 1980, a time when most gay and lesbian couples did not consider parenting to be an option even though they may have longed to have children.

But over the past decade, particularly during the past five years, a baby boom has swept gay communities in San Francisco and Boston and, to a lesser extent, in Los Angeles, New York and Seattle. The gay rights and women's movements have given rise to what is being called the gay and lesbian parenting movement. The movement, small but growing, has produced a new pioneer in the American family.

"I'm not Laura Petrie," said Schulenburg, a desktop publishing consultant who works out of her flat in a large Victorian house in San Francisco's Haight-Ashbury district. "I'm me and I wanted desperately to have a child. People ask: 'Won't it be hard for your kid? Aren't you setting your child up for a great disadvantage? Aren't you being selfish? Are you raising your kid to be gay?' My thinking all along has been that this is a wanted child, a loved child. That, to me, is a tremendous advantage."

GAY PARENTS

Gay rights groups estimate that between three million and five million homosexual parents have produced six million to eight million children in the United States. The vast majority of those children were born during traditional heterosexual unions that occurred before the parent, or parents, declared their homosexuality.

Increasingly, however, homosexuals are having children through artificial insemination, intercourse and adoption, and many are co-parenting with other lesbians or gays. By some estimates, as many as 1,000 such families reside in the San Francisco Bay Area.

"I tend to think that if you have a happy and healthy family where there's good communication, you're better off than most. It's hard to say how much more difficult this is going to be," said Ellie

112

CHILDREN OF GAY PARENTS

Researchers who have studied children of gay parents have found no evidence of harm. The timeworn prejudice that homosexuality is contagious has been all but disproved. Long-term studies have yet to be done; but there is no credible evidence that children in gay households are any more likely to be gay than children of heterosexual parents.

"Gay Parents Should Not Lose Children," **New York Times**, October, 1993

Schindelman, a 37-year- old health educator who leads support groups for lesbians considering parenthood. "All of these parents are extremely motivated," she added. "They haven't gotten pregnant by accident."

Schindelman and her lover of seven years, Kitsy, decided several years ago that they wanted to have a child, and Schindelman became pregnant through artificial insemination. Daniel Schindelman is now two years old, and they are thinking about having a second child that Kitsy would carry. (Kitsy, 33, asked that her last name not be used.) Daniel calls his parents Mama Ellie and Mama Kitsy. A legal contract stipulates that Daniel may learn his father's identity when he turns 18.

NEW GUARD

Families such as Daniel's are breaking new ground because never before in the history of the U.S. family have so many children been raised by openly gay parents. The oldest children born in this baby boom are now 10, and many parents say they are apprehensive about the approach of adolescence. "These children will face issues that will be difficult — but not insurmountable," according to Ailsa Steckel, a San Francisco psychologist who has studied some of the preschoolers.

"A determining fact will be how the parents are. What's more important than gender is the emotional health of the parents. Do the parents allow the child to wonder and to be sad or angry that they don't have a father? Do the parents try to provide a male role model? Do they feel secure in their own choices, and can they help the child deal with prejudice in other people?"

RESEARCH

About 12 studies comparing children of lesbian parents and children of heterosexual parents have suggested that the lesbians' children do not differ in development of their sexual identity and show no greater preference for homosexuality, Steckel said.

Research also has concluded that children of gay parents are more affected by their parents' divorce, or the unavailability of the absent parent in a divorce, than by the disclosure of a parent's homosexuality.

"We don't have secrets. I think that's the big difference between our family and the families that came before us," said Schulenburg, who cares for Veronica with two gay men whom the child calls Daddy and Papa. Both men were with Schulenburg when she gave birth, and both are listed on Veronica's birth certificate, one as husband and the other as biological father. Veronica has taken her fathers' names. She is Veronica Lacquement-Worcester. Veronica interrupts her finger-painting, and offers: "I love having two dads. It's funner with two dads than one. You get to play more with them. It's just normal. I wish I had two moms."

FILM

In the documentary film "Not All Parents Are Straight", Leslie, 16, recalls how she felt when her father told her he was gay: "I thought, God, this is so weird. This is something you read about in the *National Enquirer*. At first I was really hurt and I was ashamed of him. I was really disgusted. I didn't know what it meant."

Leslie's response wasn't unusual, according to Marty Carls, who counsels children of gay parents. "The older a kid is, it's more difficult to accept — not that Dad is gay but that Dad has lied to them," he said. "Not that being gay isn't sometimes a shock to them and a fear factor, but the main thing is: You lied to me."

San Francisco filmmaker Kevin White, 32, produced "Not All Parents Are Straight". White's father, a retired physician, declared his homosexuality when White was 16. His mother fell in love with a woman a few years later.

"It was a curse because there was no normalcy to it," he said, "but it was a blessing because I got to experience something very different than most people and I was able to see adults making difficult choices. It was painful but to be otherwise wouldn't have been truthful."

The children in "Not All Parents Are Straight" say that telling friends they have a gay parent is one of the most difficult things they face. They choose their friends carefully, and they resent most of all when they are judged by their parent's sexuality.

WORKSHOPS

In San Francisco, there are workshops for lesbians considering parenthood, for lesbians ready to get pregnant, for gay men and lesbians who want to parent together and for new gay parents. There are discussion groups on raising children and choosing child care, and there are play groups and organized events for children of gay parents.

The Minneapolis Public Schools have offered parenting classes for gays and lesbians for a year now. School officials say enrollment has been holding steady at seven to 10 couples per quarter. One woman drove weekly from Fargo, N.D., to attend classes.

The classes are operated by the district's Early Childhood Family Education program and meet in the Jefferson School, 1200 W. 26th St., Minneapolis. For information call 627-2927. "You can live here or in Boston and you know you won't be the first in your PTA, the first in your play group or the first in your child-care center," said Schindelman. "It's a young movement but it's growing."

"I can tell you there are a lot of parents of 10-year-olds who are definitely worried about what comes next because we don't know what's going to happen. We're still building a history."

21   THE GAY FAMILY

HOMOSEXUALS SHOULD NOT HAVE PARENTAL RIGHTS

Human Events

The following article appeared in Human Events, *a weekly conservative publication based in Washington, D.C.*

Points to Consider:

1. Summarize objections of the following article to state courts placing children with homosexual parents.

2. Cite weaknesses of research data concerning homosexual parents.

3. Analyze Kirkpatrick's statement: "I don't think it [raising healthy children] depends as much on the structure of the family as on the function of the family."

4. How might a child from a homosexual home be likened to a child from an abusive home?

"Homosexuals Push for Parental Rights," **Human Events**, December 7, 1991. Reprinted with permission.

Most Americans would hasten to reject governmental authorization of homosexual parenting.

America's homosexual activists have as their eventual goal the complete legitimization of homosexuality in every sphere of life. While many Americans have noted their efforts to place homosexual behavior under the protection of the civil rights laws, probably not many are aware that these same activists have turned their eyes on the family itself — specifically, the rearing of children — as an area to press for equal legal status with heterosexuals.

Thus, added to the usual demands for the legalization of homosexual marriage, we are now seeing a push towards legalized homosexual adoption of children.

THE COURTS

In addition, some state courts have ordered placement of children with homosexual parents who are involved in custody disputes with their estranged heterosexual spouses. Judges have also ordered children into homosexual foster homes and, even more bizarre, lesbians have taken to having themselves artificially inseminated so as to have their own children — sometimes as part of an agreement with a homosexual male friend to use his semen in exchange for handing over to him a second child.

Whatever state courts and homosexual activists may be quietly doing, however, most Americans would hasten to reject governmental authorization of homosexual parenting, seeing such family arrangements as perverse and, in an age of AIDS and pedophilia, more dangerous than ever before. At the least, most would harbor fears for the psychic health of children reared in such an environment.

Indeed, most would probably echo the words of former Supreme Court Chief Justice Warren Burger, who wrote in upholding the constitutionality of Georgia's anti-sodomy statute in 1986, "Condemnation of homosexuality is firmly rooted in Judeo-Christian moral and ethical standards." Notwithstanding such High Court judgments, however, the battle still rages across the country.

SCIENTIFIC STUDIES

In trying to further their cause, a favorite tactic of homosexual activists is to invoke allegedly "scientific" studies that purport to

PARENTAL BEHAVIOR

In almost every area, parental behavior has a profound, at times predominant, impact on children. The children of smokers frequently become smokers. Kids from abusive homes often become abusers. Children from broken homes are more likely to divorce. Only in the case of homosexuality are we asked to believe that what happens in the home is irrelevant to emotional development.

Don Feder, "Dangers of Gay Parenting Are Underrated," **Creators Syndicate,** September 27, 1993

demonstrate that homosexuals make fine parents and that they have been unfairly treated by courts and adoption agencies for years.

Nor surprisingly, California is the state where such arguments have been most widely accepted, though judges and governmental authorities in other states have begun to show signs of subscribing to the same "enlightened" doctrines. A recent *Los Angeles Times* article by Scott Harris on the topic of homosexual parenting is the latest salvo directed at those Americans whose common sense and moral beliefs lead them to reject such legal innovations out of hand.

Harris' lengthy apologia for homosexual parenting drew heavily on the work of UCLA's Dr. Martha Kirkpatrick. Indeed, Harris himself told *Human Events* that Kirkpatrick's studies of children reared by lesbians provided the foundation for his article. He quotes Kirkpatrick's conclusion: "Whatever goes on in a family has an effect on the child. But we cannot find, by the current measures available, that any evidence of homosexuality in a parent has a specific detrimental effect on a child." Kirkpatrick also says that children reared by homosexuals do not show any increased tendency to become homosexuals themselves.

Elsewhere Harris notes, "Judges, persuaded by growing research data that gays are as able as heterosexuals to be worthy parents, have increasingly granted gays custody of children and approved adoption by gays."

FAULTY RESEARCH

But how reliable are such research data? A careful reading of Kirkpatrick's monograph, "Homosexuality and Parenting", reveals

118

that, far from having clinched the case in favor of such families, scientific studies of the phenomenon are in their infancy and are conducted with the crudest of research methods. One such method is the Toy Preference Test in which inferences are drawn about a mother's influence on a child's acquisition of a sex role based on what toys his mother would choose for him.

Even more disquieting for anyone hoping to rely on the research of Kirkpatrick and others in the field is her own admission that absolutely no long-term studies (termed "longitudinal studies" in the jargon of researchers) have been conducted to determine if children reared in homosexual homes grow up to be well adjusted.

Studies of children reared in homosexual homes from birth are only just now getting underway; such studies as have been done have focused on children reared by divorced lesbians, etc. No follow-up studies have been done even of the mothers and children who have been subjected to some testing by researchers. Kirkpatrick herself lamented to us on the phone that the frequent moving around of her subjects made such follow-up studies virtually impossible.

Furthermore, according to Kirkpatrick, the research done on homosexual males as parents is even more sparse than that done on lesbians as child rearers. Kirkpatrick, whose study group numbered only 20, told us that she once served on the board of directors of National Gay Rights Advocates, but she stressed that she had gotten involved with the advocacy group only after she had begun doing research in the field and had decided homosexual parenting posed no risks for children.

THE FAMILY

"I don't think we know the best way to raise healthy children," Kirkpatrick told us, "but I don't think it depends as much on the structure of the family as on the function of the family. I don't think it depends on the sexual orientation of the parents or kinship relationship between those caring for the children, the amount of money they have, or whether a father is present. In my mind all these things are less important than whether the family as a unit feels comfortable with each other, is supportive and respectful, and deals openly about disagreements."

Nevertheless, even Kirkpatrick concedes that her research showed that many children, when informed of their mother's homosexuality, were "shocked, confused, hurt and embarrassed. Young children need to deny the meaning of the information; older children may be burdened by the secret or have concerns for their own sexual development, with an increased pressure to act out their heterosexuality for reassurance."

Despite her repeated claims to *Times* reporter Harris and to us that the sexual orientation of parents was relatively unimportant, her "Homosexuality and Parenting" ends by cautioning, "We cannot assume that a parent's homosexuality has no effect on a child, only that the effects are variable in direction and extent, and there is specific or inevitable effect." This is well short of a clear scientific statement that a judge could rely on in deciding, for example, a custody case.

RESEARCH

Not surprisingly, there are some researchers who downplay the significance of the work of Kirkpatrick and other students of homosexual parenting. Dr. Judith Reisman, author of *Kinsey, Sex and Fraud* and *"Softporn" Plays Hardball*, reaffirmed to *Human Events* that there was insufficient data to come to any conclusions on the topic, and termed the *Los Angeles Times* article "a puff piece".

"You have a broad spectrum of detrimental effects," said Riesman about children brought up by homosexuals. She said that those detrimental effects were widely recognized in the medical community until it became "politically incorrect" to mention them. To state only the most obvious and easily checked problems," she added, "homosexual men have the highest rates of all communicable diseases — hepatitis, tuberculosis, etc."

She said, "We do know what makes for healthy children: a mom and a dad with an extended family to provide backup if parents get sick, or have financial problems, etc. It is simply true to say that we take better care of our kin than of others."

Reisman pointed with horror to a recent study in the *Journal of Sex Research* indicating that "31 percent of lesbians and 12 percent of homosexual males reported being victims of forced sex by their current or most recent partner," with battery being part of the coercion involved. "You've got a lot of angry people in these groups," Reisman said, "and it's frightening to think of this violence being visited on children, particularly in a sexual context."

120

PEDOPHILES

The potential for abuse by pedophiles was a major concern of Reisman. "Children are not guinea pigs to be experimented with," she said, and advised interested readers to look at the advertisements in the back of homosexual magazines for evidence of how widespread a desire for "young people" is among homosexuals.

She said that she feared that male pedophiles would increase their desire for children as the AIDS epidemic worsened because they are thought to be safe, and warned that a Duke University Department of Pediatrics report states that 14 percent of children with AIDS were identified as victims of sexual abuse.

"You won't learn about that from the *L.A. Times* article," she added ruefully.

RECOGNIZING AUTHOR'S POINT OF VIEW

This activity may be used as an individualized study guide for students in libraries and resource centers or as a discussion catalyst in small group and classroom discussions.

Guidelines

Good readers make clear distinctions between descriptive articles that relate factual information and articles that express a point of view. Articles that express editorial commentary and analysis are featured in this publication. Examine the following statements. Then try to decide if any of these statements take a similar position to any of the authors in Chapter Four. Working as individuals or in small groups, try to match the point of view in each statement below with the most appropriate author in Chapter Four. Mark the appropriate reading number in front of each statement. Mark (O) for any statement that cannot be associated with the point of view or any reading in Chapter Four.

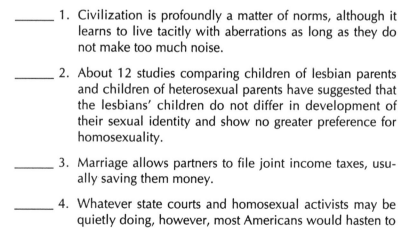

_____ 1. Civilization is profoundly a matter of norms, although it learns to live tacitly with aberrations as long as they do not make too much noise.

_____ 2. About 12 studies comparing children of lesbian parents and children of heterosexual parents have suggested that the lesbians' children do not differ in development of their sexual identity and show no greater preference for homosexuality.

_____ 3. Marriage allows partners to file joint income taxes, usually saving them money.

_____ 4. Whatever state courts and homosexual activists may be quietly doing, however, most Americans would hasten to reject government authorization of homosexual parenting, seeing such family arrangements as perverse and, in an age of AIDS and pedophilia, more dangerous than ever before.

_____ 5. With regard to marriage, whether homosexual behavior is a choice or not is irrelevant, since one's marriage partner is always a matter of choice.

_____ 6. A careful reading of Kirkpatrick's monograph, "Homosexuality and Parenting", reveals that, far from having clinched the case in favor of such families, scientific studies of the phenomenon are in their infancy and are conducted with the crudest of research methods.

_____ 7. The demand for "gay rights" extends much further. It involves, as I understand it, the legislation of homosexual marriage. It involves the "right" of homosexual couples to adopt children, and so forth.

_____ 8. None of the recent thirty-five studies on homosexual parents has shown that parental sexual orientation has any adverse effect on children (and that the children of gays are no more likely to be gay themselves).

_____ 9. In trying to further their cause, a tactic of homosexual activists is to invoke allegedly "scientific" studies that purport to demonstrate that homosexuals make fine parents and that they have been unfairly treated by courts and adoption agencies for years.

_____10. To accord homosexual relations a legal presumption of normality would be something new in human history, and, if only on that account, something of which to be extremely wary.

_____11. Society already has a measure of relational union — it's called marriage, and it's not at all difficult to ascertain: either you're married or you're not.

_____12. Families are breaking new ground because never before in the history of the U.S. family have so many children been raised by openly gay parents.

_____13. We do know what makes for healthy children: a mom and a dad with an extended family to provide backup if parents get sick, or have financial problems.

CHAPTER 5

THE GAY RIGHTS MOVEMENT

22   THE GAY RIGHTS MOVEMENT

GAYS AND LESBIANS WANT EQUALITY

Jennifer Juarez Robles

Jennifer Juarez Robles is an editorial writer for the Star Tribune *of Minneapolis.*

Points to Consider:

1. What traditionally have been the two choices for people regarding their homosexuality?

2. Contrast the conservative and the militant view of homosexuals and society.

3. Define "full civil equality" as it relates to homosexuals.

4. How might society best be persuaded about the worth of homosexuals?

Jennifer Juarez Robles, "What Gays and Lesbians Want Is Not Approval But Equality," **Star Tribune**, Minneapolis, July, 1993. Reprinted by permission of the **Star Tribune**, Minneapolis.

Something is abnormally wrong with prevailing society when it causes parents to reject sons and daughters due to a condition that is largely, if not entirely, involuntary.

This is the day my mother rues — Pride Day. The annual parade and festival celebrate lesbian, gay, bisexual and transgender people. "Why do you have to flaunt it?" she always asks me, but it's really not a question. My mother subscribes to the Senator Sam Nunn philosophy: "Don't ask, don't tell," with marked emphasis on the "don't tell."

GAY RIGHTS

We have managed over the years to establish a wary truce about my lesbianism — we don't talk about it, which, believe it or not, is an improvement over the intense confrontations we used to have. She does not participate in my lesbian life so it's no surprise that my mother never has come to terms with the annual June remembrance of the Stonewall riots.

She is ashamed by the public display of homosexuality and its attendant drag queens and leather folk who have historically occupied media broadcasts, and thus the majority's viewpoint, of Pride Day and, by extension, homosexuality. She is not alone in her discomfort. Her challenge, like that of much of mainstream America, is to see the trees as well as the forest. Too often, the gay experience is homogenized and individual lives subsumed. Additionally, many in the gay political movement wrongly believe that it is their mission to gain private tolerance of homosexuality.

Despite our tactical silence, my mother has sometimes supported the struggle for gay rights. She has rallied recently to the defense of gays in the military, believing that Nunn's hearings only exposed the feebleness of the military's position. "How could they kick out Jose Zuniga, who was Soldier of the Year?" she asked after the March on Washington. "He's a good soldier. Who cares if he's gay?"

MIDDLE CLASS VALUES

What troubles my mother about Pride Day is the assault on her middle-class values, "the exhibitionism" that, to her, goes beyond social acceptance to social upheaval. My mother reflects what Andrew Sullivan of the *New Republic* calls the "moderate politics of homosexuality", which he defines as people who "do not want persecution of homosexuals, but they do not want overt approval

126

either."

This is an old, unresolved concern, even among gays and lesbians, that predates the 1969 Stonewall riots that many people mistakenly believe started the gay and lesbian political movement. *Stonewall*, a new book by Martin Duberman, provides valuable historical and personal context to that defining moment when drag queens, lesbians and gay men in New York City fought a police raid on the Stonewall Inn. Mafia-owned, the bar regularly paid for police protection but may have angered federal officials by selling bootlegged liquor. Next year marks the 25th anniversary of the riots.

MODERN MOVEMENTS

Duberman traces the roots of the modern gay liberation movement to such organizations as the Mattachine Society and the Daughters of Bilitis, both of which began in the 1950s. Even then fierce debates centered on whether gays and lesbians were better off adopting a conservative, assimilationist path or one which relied on an aggressive, political struggle. One path favored a "don't ask, don't tell" compromise, the other required people to come out of the closet.

CIVIL RIGHTS

Civil rights for lesbians and gay men is an issue of social justice. Lesbians and gays do not currently enjoy the same rights and freedoms most Americans take for granted. It is time the civil and human rights that form the foundation of this country be universally applied to all people.

"Why Should You Support Lesbian and Gay Rights?" **National Organization for Women** Position Paper, 1991

Writes Duberman: "In 1964-65, New York Mattachine was still controlled by the conservatives. They believed in gradualism and quietism, in modifying gay comportment so that it would better coincide with middle-class notions of proper behavior, in concentrating on education, in allying with and relying on whatever sympathetic experts they could find in straight religious, legal, and psychiatric circles.

"Where the conservatives emphasized the need for the homosexual to adjust to society, the militants, taking their cue from the black civil rights struggle, insisted that society had to do the adjusting, had to stop belittling and persecuting gay people."

The Stonewall riots tipped the scales in favor of nonconformity, political activism and the encouragement of open homosexuality. Yet 24 years later, after important social and political improvements, particularly in the psychoanalytic and medical fields, the question of how far the gay movement should go still is a central one. But the gay movement must rely less on politics and more on the transforming power of openly gay and lesbian individuals in other spheres.

My mother doesn't want legislated morality that would force her to adopt the slogan of the early gay rights movement that "Gay is good." She doesn't want to give her seal of approval to homosexuality, which she sees as a Pride Day demand. She won't accept the requirement that she embrace drag queens, bull dykes or any of the other horrid stereotypes that keep parents at arm's length from their children.

CIVIL RIGHTS

I've got news for her. I don't need anyone, especially my mother, to approve of my homosexuality. All I want is the benefits that het-

ANTIGAY CRIMES

Reports of gay bashing and other bias crimes against gays surged an average of 31 percent in five major cities in the past year. The National Gay and Lesbian Task Force Policy Institute, a gay rights group based in Washington, said 1,822 criminal incidents, ranging from verbal harassment to murder, were reported by gay victim assistance programs in New York City, Boston, Chicago, the Twin Cities and San Francisco.

Lida Poletz, "Antigay Crimes Rise 31 Percent," **Star Tribune** of Minneapolis, March 20, 1992

erosexuals automatically receive by living in a public state. I'm holding out for "full civil equality" — as Sullivan says, "that all public (as opposed to private) discrimination against homosexuals be ended and that every right and responsibility that heterosexuals enjoy by virtue of the state be extended to those who grow up different."

In other words, allow gay marriages and openly gay people in the military as fruits of living in a civil, public society. But don't legislate private tolerance. I will continue to oppose my mother's disapproval of my homosexuality on cultural, moral or religious grounds. Yet I respect her position that the gay liberation movement should not seek to govern traditional, heterosexual values.

Rather, let our individual, openly gay lives persuade others of our societal worth. The story of "Stonewall" is told in unique fashion through six people who participated in the first remembrance of the riots in 1970. The stories of a Latino drag queen, a black lesbian, three white gay men and one white lesbian are all remarkably different yet similar in their childhood difficulties, survival mechanisms and social and political activism.

TOLERANCE

None of the "Stonewall" activists ever had adult ties with their families, a fact that should not go unnoticed. For something is abnormally wrong with prevailing society when it causes parents to reject sons and daughters due to a condition that is largely, if not entirely, involuntary.

Yet rectifying that abnormality is not solely a governmental responsibility. It is the duty of all lesbian and gay people to come out to their parents and the greater society. "Do tell" is a better prescription against private intolerance, and a freer one at that.

My fervent wish is that my mother and I will someday march in a Pride Parade with PFLAG, the supportive organization of parents and friends of lesbians and gays. Yet I don't altogether need the government or the gay movement to legislate my mother's tolerance. I will win that on my own.

23   THE GAY RIGHTS MOVEMENT

HOMOSEXUALITY IS NOT A CIVIL RIGHT

Family Research Council

The following article is excerpted from In Focus, *a publication of the Family Research Council, a Washington, D.C.-based organization which promotes conservative ideals and values.*

Points to Consider:

1. How might barring homosexuals from military service be seen in the same light as barring older people?

2. How does the homosexual population fit the three criteria characterizing minorities?

3. Why might homosexual activists avoid public discussion of homosexual behavior?

4. How might homosexual marriage undermine the traditional institutions of marriage and family?

Robert H. Knight, "Homosexuality Is Not a Civil Right," **In Focus**, 1993. Reprinted by permission of Robert H. Knight, Director of Cultural Studies, Family Research Council in Washington, D.C.

Homosexuals do not need special protection.

In an attempt to gain acceptance and special protection for their behavior, homosexual activists seek to hijack the moral capital of the civil rights movement.

CIVIL RIGHTS

Essential to the homosexual agenda is the idea that homosexuals are fighting for basic civil rights denied them by an oppressive society. This argument strikes a sympathetic chord among many Americans, whose decency and sense of fair play demand that all people be treated fairly.

However, a closer look at the truth about homosexuality and the political goals of the "gay rights" movement shows that homosexuals are not an oppressed minority, that opposition to special protection for homosexuality is not bigotry and that extending such protection is dangerous to individuals and society.

Contrary to their claims of "discrimination", there is no effort to deny homosexuals the same rights guaranteed to all Americans. The truth is that homosexuals have the same rights, with the same restrictions, as everyone else. Homosexuals have the right to free speech, freedom of religion, due process under the law, the right to engage in commerce, to enter into contracts, own property, vote, along with a host of other rights. In fact, an ACLU handbook lists dozens of rights homosexuals already enjoy.[1] In this country all citizens are guaranteed equal protection under the law. Homosexuals do not need special protection.

Homosexuals are barred from military service as are a dozen other groups, such as older people, young people, single parents, and others who detract from the military's mission. Military service is not a right but a privilege and a duty for some.

A TRUE MINORITY

The notion that homosexuals are a true minority group is false. Homosexuals don't meet the three criteria that characterize minority groups that have been accorded special protections.

1. Economic Deprivation. Homosexuals are among the most advantaged people in our country. Research by marketing firms shows that homosexuals as a group:

I DENY EVER SUGGESTING LIMITATIONS ON GAYS IN COMBAT ROLES. ON THE CONTRARY, I'VE GREAT RESPECT FOR GAYS' (UN) MARTIAL SKILLS.

Henry Paine. Reprinted by permission of United Features Syndicate, Inc.

- Have higher than average per-capita annual incomes ($36,800 vs $12,287) and higher than average household incomes ($55,430 vs $32,144).

- Are more likely to hold advanced degrees (59.6% vs 18%).

- Are more likely to hold professional or managerial positions (49% vs 15.9%).

- Are more likely to be overseas travelers and frequent flyers.[2]

2. Political Powerlessness. Homosexuals display political power far beyond their numbers. This tiny group, about 1% of the population,[3] donated $3 million to the Clinton-Gore campaign.[4] They have one of the largest and fastest growing Political Action Committees in Washington, D.C.[5] The Human Rights Campaign Fund donated $4.5 million to candidates last year, more than almost any non-corporate PAC.[6]

Openly homosexual politicians hold various high public offices in urban areas such as San Francisco and New York. In addition, homosexuals enjoy support from every major news organization, whose coverage long ago crossed the line into outright advocacy of homosexual causes.

3. Immutable Characteristics. Minority groups share immutable, benign, non-behavioral characteristics such as race, ethnicity, disability or national origin. Homosexuals are the only group to claim minority status based on behavior. There is no reliable scientific evidence which shows that homosexual behavior is biological in origin. A recent, comprehensive examination of genetic claims for homosexuality in the *Archives of General Psychiatry* (March, 1993) concludes, "There is no evidence at present to substantiate a biologic theory..."[7] Also, the existence of thousands of people who have come out of the homosexual lifestyle shows that homosexuality is not immutable.

SPECIAL INTEREST GROUP

Rather than being considered a minority group, homosexuals are more accurately described as a special interest group. But even that description may be overly generous. Unlike lobbies such as the Association of Trial Lawyers of America and the Realtors Political Action Committee, which represent legitimate concerns, homosexuals are pressing for government-enforced approval of activities that have been condemned in all successful cultures as immoral, unhealthy and destructive to individuals and societies.

Using civil rights arguments is an exploitation of good people's sympathy. A 1987 article in the homosexual magazine *Guide* outlines the strategy homosexuals should use to gain special protection: "In any campaign to win over the public, gays must be cast as victims in need of protection so that straights will be inclined by reflex to assume the role of protector...Our campaign should not demand direct support for homosexual practices, but should instead take anti-discrimination as its theme."[8]

HOMOSEXUAL ACTIVISTS

Indeed, homosexual activists actively avoid public discussion of homosexual behavior. In the 1989 book *After the Ball: How America Will Conquer Its Hatred and Fear of Homosexuals in the 90s*, a blueprint for homosexual political power, the authors warn that: "The public should not be shocked and repelled by premature exposure to homosexual behavior itself."[9]

Homosexual activists realize that when people become aware of common homosexual practices, such as anal intercourse, anal-oral contact[10] — along with other homosexual practices such as inserting arms inside each others bodies and "sports" involving bodily excre-

HOMOSEXUAL ACTIVISTS

Homosexual activists tend to frame their demands in classic civil rights language. They seek only an end to discrimination, they claim. That includes discrimination in the military and in marriage and adoption laws, which currently require that spouses be of different genders.

Mona Charen, "What Do Homosexual Activists Really Want?" **Creators Syndicate, Inc.**, 1993

tions — they will see that these behaviors do not merit special protection in our laws.

Granting special protection to homosexual behavior would also harm civil society by undermining the institutions of marriage and family. Throughout the world, marriage and family are held in highest esteem. They are recognized as the foundations for civil society. The value and benefit of marriage and family as the genesis of each new generation are reflected in our nation's laws, which afford them special protections and benefits. If homosexual behavior were to receive the same status, marriage and family would be reduced to just one of a number of lifestyle choices. The effort to redefine the family is really an effort to destroy the common definition and has no logical stopping point. If marriage no longer means the union of a man and a woman, then why not "marry" three men, or two men and a woman? Putting homosexual behavior on a par with marriage and family sends the wrong message to a nation already overburdened with family breakdown and its attendant pathologies.

SPECIAL PROTECTION

Granting special protection to homosexuals would also take away rights from others. Parents would lose the rights to protect their children from exposure to homosexuality. Private religious and civic groups would no longer be able to exclude homosexuals. The Boy Scouts of America are being sued in several states for refusing to admit homosexuals. These attacks on the Scouts convey the message that parents will no longer be free to ensure that organizations to whom they entrust their children will convey the parents' values. That is tyranny masquerading as tolerance.

Landlords, even those in duplexes and family-centered complexes, could be forced to rent to open homosexuals.

135

CONCLUSION

Opposition to extending special protection to homosexuals is not based on ignorance or bigotry. It is based on informed judgment about homosexual behavior and the political agenda of homosexual activists. If pro-family concerns were not based on fact, logic and careful thought, we might indeed be guilty of prejudice. But we know that homosexual behavior is unhealthy. We know that homosexuals are much more likely to contract AIDS[11] and a host of other sexually transmitted diseases.[12] We know that homosexuals typically have shorter lifespans[13] and that they are more likely to have drug and alcohol abuse problems.[14] These things are personal tragedies but are hardly the basis for granting special civil rights protection.

Communities have an obligation to discourage, not encourage, destructive behavior. Compassion dictates that we do no less. Saying "no" to homosexual activities is not bigotry; it is common sense.

ENDNOTES

[1] Nan D. Hunter, Sherryl E. Michaelson, Thomas B. Stoddard, *The Rights of Lesbians and Gay Men: The Basic ACLU Guide to a Gay Person's Rights*, Third Edition, Southern Illinois University Press, Carbondale and Edwardsville, 1992.

[2] "Overview of the Simmons Gay Media Survey," Rivendell Marketing Company, Plainfield, New Jersey, undated, p.1. See also: Dennis Kneale, "Gay Consumer Spending," *The Wall Street Journal*, February 10, 1989; Trish Hall, "For Gay Travelers, More Places to Go," *The New York Times*, August 22, 1990, p. C-1; Iris Cohen Selinger, "Survey Verifies Affluence of Gays," *Adweek*, February 27, 1989, p. 73.

[3] John O.G. Billy, Koray Tanfer, William R. Grady and Daniel H. Klepinger, "The Sexual Behavior of Men in the United States," *Family Planning Perspectives*, Vol. 25, No. 2, March/April 1993. See also, J. Gordon Muir, "Homosexuals and the 10% Fallacy," *The Wall Street Journal*, March 31, 1993, p. A-14.

[4] Adam Nagourney, "Homophiliac," *The New Republic*, January 4 and 11, 1993, p. 16.

[5] John Anderson, "Top 50 PACS," *The Washington Post*, June 8, 1992, p. A-17.

[6] "Homosexual Politics After AIDS," *The Economist*, April 24, 1993, pp. 26-27.

[7] William Byne and Bruce Parsons, "Human Sexual Orientation: The Biologic Theories Reappraised," *The Archives of General Psychiatry*, Vol. 50, March 1993, pp. 228-239.

[8] Marshall K. Kirk & Erastes Pill, "The Overhauling of Straight America," *Guide Magazine*, November 1987, pp. 7-14.

[9] Marshall Kirk and Hunter Madsen, *After the Ball: How America Will Conquer Its Hatred and Fear of Homosexuals in the '90's.* Bantam Doubleday Dell Publishing Group Inc., New York, NY, 1989, pp. 177-178.

[10] A.P. Bell and M.S. Wienberg, *Homosexualities: A Study of Diversity Among Men and Women*, Simon and Schuster, New York, 1978, pp. 308-309; Karla Jay and Allen Young, *The Gay Report*, Summit, New York, 1979; Jeffrey A. Kelly, et al., "Acquired Immunodeficiency Syndrome / Human Immunodeficiency Virus Risk Behavior Among Gay Men in Small Cities; Findings of a 16-City National Sample," *Archives of Internal Medicine*, Vol. 152, November 1992, pp. 2293-2297.

[11] "The HIV/AIDS Surveillance Report," U.S. Department of Health and Human Services, Centers for Disease Control, National Center for Infectious Diseases, Division of HIV/AIDS, February 1993, p. 10.

[12] H.W. Jaffee, and C. Keewhan, et al., "National Case-Control Study of Kaposi's Sarcoma and Pneumocystis Carinii Pneumonia in Homosexual Men; Part 1, Epidemiological Results," *Annals of Internal Medicine*, 1983, 99 (2) pp. 145-147; H.H. Hansfield, "Sexually Transmitted Disease in Homosexual Men," *American Journal of Public Health*, 9, 1981, pp. 989-990; Karla Jay and Allen Young, *The Gay Report*, Summit, New York, 1979; Janet E. Gans, et al., "America's Adolescents: How Healthy Are They?" American Medical Association, 1990, p. 31.

[13] Paul Cameron, William I. Playfair, and Stephen Wellum, "The Homosexual Lifespan," Family Research Institute, Inc., Washington, D.C. 1992.

[14] "Gays Are More Prone to Substance Abuse," *Insight*, November 5, 1990.

24   THE GAY RIGHTS MOVEMENT

THE GAY MOMENT

Andrew Kopkind

Andrew Kopkind is an associate editor of The Nation, *a weekly liberal magazine of social and political opinion based in New York City.*

Points to Consider:

1. Why has "outing" made life as a homosexual better than ever before in America?

2. Why is Colorado being called the "hate state"?

3. Describe the Christian Right's response to homosexuality.

4. In what institutions might "the closet" be seen as maintaining order?

Every opinion survey shows that people who say they have a gay friend or family member are two or three times as likely to support gay rights than are those who say they know no gay people.

Newspapers censor pro-gay comic strips, television stations ban gay programs, schools proscribe gay-positive materials, church hierarchs forbid gay people from preaching — and parading, state electorates revoke existing anti-discrimination laws and outlaw passage of new ones, and bullies on streets of every city beat and bash gays and lesbians with escalating hatred. Some 1,900 incidents of anti-gay violence were reported in 1992. Except for a small number of enlightened workplaces in college towns and the big cities of both coasts, American institutions make it dangerous or impossible for millions of gays to leave their closets and lead integrated, fulfilling lives.

THE CONTRADICTIONS

But it is the contradictions rather than the cruelties of sexual struggle that define the moment. Despite the difficulties, most gays would agree that life as a homosexual is better now than ever before in American history. The Rev. Al Carmines's hopeful but unconvincing post-Stonewall song, "I'm Gay and I'm Proud" now reflects a widespread reality. Responding to the rigidity of the old order, younger gay men and "baby dykes" have created a queer culture that is rapidly reconfiguring American values, redesigning sensibilities and remodeling politics. The gay movement, broadly construed, is the movement of the moment. Devastated by a plague that threatens the very existence of their community, gay men have converted horror and grief into creative energy and purpose. AIDS has given a new sense of solidarity to lesbians and gay men who for years have often pursued separate agendas. Broadway is bursting with gay plays, big book awards go to gay authors, even Hollywood is developing movies with gay themes, and gay people of every age and social stratum are shattering their closets with explosive force. "Queer theory" — also known as lesbian and gay studies — is explored by scholars and students at hundreds of colleges.

Suddenly, "out" gays inhabit high and mid-level positions in journalism and publishing, law, academia, medicine and psychiatry, the arts and creative professions. They have made it not only possible, but comfortable and natural for younger lesbians and gay men to come out at the entry level. More out gays are in public office throughout the land, at least up to the sub-Cabinet level of the federal government. A quarter of a century of gay and lesbian political action has produced, *inter alia*, the first pro-gay White House — despite distressing backsliding. Gay couples are winning recognition as legal families by some city governments and a few corporations (*The Nation* is one), although valuable benefits have been extended to only a small number of registrants. And a complex infrastructure of activist, educational and professional organizations give gay life a formidable institutional base and contribute to the general appreciation of "gay power". Morley Safer was not way over the top when he suggested to his "60 Minutes" audience that it "face up to the gay nineties."

Ten years ago there might have been one gay issue in the news every month or so. Now there are dozens at the same time. The tortured topic of gays in the military is far from the "nonstarter" the late Bush re-election campaign, incredibly, assumed it to be. It strikes at the authority of the defense establishment in political life and, on a deeper level, subverts traditional gender and sexual roles as no movement has done since the dawn of modern feminism.

STATE REFERENDUMS

In the aftermath of Colorado's passage of Amendment 2, making it illegal for the state or any locality to protect gays from assaults on their civil rights, Christian fundamentalist churches and other right-wing groups are mounting campaigns for retrograde referendums in a dozen states, many of which had already enacted antidiscrimination laws for gays after exhausting campaigns. (Target states: Idaho, Oregon, California and Florida.) Gays and, for the first time, a significant number of straight allies are pushing a boycott of the "hate state" of Colorado. William Rubenstein, the American Civil Liberties Union point man on gay issues, marvels at the broadening of anger against homophobia. "The kind of outrage that Barbara Streisand and other celebrities are registering on gay issues has simply never been seen before."

Gays start at a disadvantage in resources. The fundamentalists can mobilize literally millions of people in a few days to phone or fax Congress and send money to anti-gay campaigns. There are perhaps 1,200 radio and TV outlets operated by religious broadcasters that may be available for homophobic propaganda and fundraising. Now that international communism is a dead issue, and abortion is no longer a leading edge, homosexuality is the Christian right's number one bogey and its chief source of money.

Cartoon by Gary Markstein. Reprinted by permission of **The Milwaukee Journal.**

During the campaign around the Oregon gay-rights proposition last year, Christian militants produced a sensationalist video called "The Gay Agenda", which is up there with the Nazi film "The Eternal Jew" as a work of pure hate and fear. The video has had saturation distribution. The Joint Chiefs of Staff showed it to one another (their response to the expanse of male flesh and repeated crotch shots is unrecorded) and passed it on to members of Congress. One general personally sent it to Representative Pat Schroeder, who blasted back an angry public reply. A group of filmmakers in New York City, working as the Gay and Lesbian Emergency Media Campaign, is trying to rush out countervideos, but it's hard to drive really bad politics out with good...

THE CLOSET

What has changed the climate in America is the long experience of gay struggle, the necessary means having been, first, coming out, and second, making a scene. Sometimes it is personal witness, other times political action, and overall it is the creation of a cultural community based on sexual identity.

The ascension of gay people to positions of authority in key sectors of society has made a huge difference in the weather. The prerequisite for their influence is being out — which is why the destruction of the closet is the most vital issue of gay life, beyond any act of censorship or exclusion. It is also the reason that "outing" has become such a charged political question.

Every opinion survey shows that people who say they have a gay friend or family member are two or three times as likely to support gay rights than are those who say they know no gay people. What the surveys don't report is the opinion of people who know out gays. None of the events and activities listed above — the political victories, the cultural successes achieved by gays in the past short period of time — would have been possible if closets were shut.

The military establishment, schools, churches all understand the importance of the closet in maintaining institutional order. That is why the services never cared a damn about gays who did not proclaim their identity, by word or deed. It is why school superintendents have lived for centuries with lesbian and gay teachers, but panic when anyone comes out. It's why churches countenance lesbian nuns and gay priests and ministers as long as they lie about themselves.

Andrew Sullivan wrote recently in *The New York Times* that dropping the military ban on gays would be a deeply conservative act, in that gays who join up would be, by definition, patriotic and traditionalist. That may be true in the particular, but in general and historical terms, nothing could be more radical than upsetting the sexual apple cart. The patriarchal power of the military consists precisely in the sexual status quo, and when gays become visible they undercut that power. Randy Shilts asserts in his study of gays in the service, *Conduct Unbecoming*, "The presence of gay men [in the military]...calls into question everything that manhood is supposed to mean." And homophobia — like its blood relations, racism, misogyny and anti-Semitism — is an ideology that rationalizes the oppressive uses of male power. When cruel and self-hating homophobes such as J. Edgar Hoover and Roy Cohn are outed, even posthumously, the power system is shaken...

THE GAY NINETIES

But the gay nineties is not only about civil rights, tolerance and legitimacy. What started tumbling out of the closets at the time of Stonewall is profoundly altering the way we all live, form families, think about and act toward one another, manage our health and well-being and understand the very meaning of identity. All the crosscurrents of present-day liberation struggles are subsumed in the gay struggle. The gay moment is in some ways similar to the moment that other communities have experienced in the nation's past, but it is also something more, because sexual identity is in crisis throughout the population, and gay people — at once the most conspicuous subjects and objects of the crisis — have been forced to invent a complete cosmology to grasp it. No one says the changes will come easily. But it's just possible that a small and despised sexual minority will change America forever.

25   THE GAY RIGHTS MOVEMENT

A DUBIOUS AGENDA

Peter LaBarbera

Peter LaBarbera is the editor of the newsletter Lambda Report, *which monitors the homosexual movement.*

Points to Consider:

1. How is the Gay Agenda described?

2. What was the 1993 March demand concerning family and adoption?

3. What "weapon" do gay activists propose using against Institutional Religion?

4. What would be the purpose of desensitizing the public toward homosexuality?

Peter LaBarbera, "What Gay Activists Are Demanding," **Human Events**, May 1, 1993. Reprinted with permission.

Ultimately, homosexuals seek validation for their way of life.

Hundreds of thousands of homosexuals converged on Washington last week for the "Lesbian, Gay and Bi Equal Rights and Liberation March." The media provided supportive coverage linking the gays' cause to civil rights crusades of the past, and portrayed homosexuals as innocents just asking for a fair shake. But even as gays yearn to be counted among the mainstream, their record betrays a lifestyle and agenda far out of line with what most Americans consider normal, decent and just.

Unfortunately, much of the real homosexual agenda — and the realities of "gay" life — remains buried in the homosexual subculture to which the average American is seldom exposed.

Prominent homosexual leaders and publications have voiced support for pedophilia, incest, sadomasochism, and even bestiality. No taboo is inviolable. Gay activists routinely call for legally binding "marriage" between homosexuals — even while ridiculing traditional standards of fidelity. In fact, most Americans would be shocked to hear how loosely many gays define "monogamy".

As shown by the following quotations — all taken verbatim from the gay press and gay-authored documents — homosexuals demand that their bizarre lifestyle must be both accepted and legalized.

THE AGENDA

Much of this dubious agenda will be solidified should homosexual activists succeed in their current fight for acceptance in the U.S. military and passage of a national law that gives gays legally protected "minority" status based on their "sexual orientation".

Gay victories in these areas would put the force of law behind their sexual behavior — effectively forcing others who find homosexuality repugnant to modify their views to accommodate gays, all in the hallowed name of "civil rights".

Ultimately, homosexuals seek validation for their way of life — through the manipulation of law and culture. Their cause gains in the eyes of many Americans when it is mistakenly cast as a fight against "discrimination".

Gay activists know that the more Americans know about their real agenda and conduct, the less sympathetic they will be toward their

cause. It is easy to see why when one considers the quotations below. Let us begin with some of the demands of the gay organizers of the April 25 "March on Washington":

"Civil Rights" Bill / Repeal Sodomy Laws

"We demand passage of a Lesbian, Gay, Bisexual, and Transgender civil rights bill...; repeal of all sodomy laws and other laws that criminalize private sexual expression between consenting adults."

— *1993 March on Washington Demand #1.* [Note: "Transgender" refers to transvestites (cross dressers) and those who have had or desire sex-change operations.]

Adoptions / Redefining the Family

"We demand legislation to prevent discrimination against Lesbians, Gays, Bisexuals and Transgendered people in the areas of family diversity, custody, adoption and foster care and that the definition of family includes the full diversity of all family structures."

—*1993 March on Washington Demand #3*

Gay Curricula in Schools

"We demand full and equal inclusion of Lesbians, Gays, Bisexuals and Transgendered people in the educational system, and

146

inclusion of Lesbian, Gay, Bisexual and Transgender studies in multicultural curricula."

—1993 March on Washington Demand #4

Multiple-partner "Unions"

"Legalization of multiple partner unions."

— Demand #6 — under the "Discrimination" category — of unofficial draft list of 55 demands first put forth by the organizing committee for the 1993 March on Washington, reported in Washington Blade, *May 22, 1992.*

Pedophilia Defended

"NAMBLA's [the North American Man/Boy Love Association] position on sex is not unreasonable, just unpopular..."The love between men and boys is at the foundation of homosexuality...

— Editorial, "No Place for Homo-Homophobia," San Francisco Sentinel *(one of that city's three main gay newspapers), March 26, 1992.*

"All youth need to be provided with positive information about homosexuality that presents it as a viable adaptation. We must accept a homosexual orientation in young people in the same manner we accept a heterosexual orientation. Finally, we need to assist gay and lesbian young people in the coming out process and support them in the many conflicts they presently face."

— Paul Gibson, San Francisco social worker and gay activist, "Gay Male and Lesbian Youth Suicide", paper in HHS Task Force on Youth Suicide, January 1989, 3-134.

Gay Strategy: Undermine the Church

"...We can undermine the moral authority of homophobic churches by portraying them as antiquated backwaters, badly out of step with the times and with the latest findings of psychology. Against the mighty pull of Institutional Religion, one must set the mightier draw of Science and Public Opinion (the shield and sword of that accursed 'secular humanism'). Such an unholy alliance has worked well against the church before, on such topics as divorce and abortion. With enough open talk about the prevalence and acceptability of homosexuality, that alliance can work again here."

— Marshall Kirk and Erastes Pill, "The Overhauling of Straight

America," Guide Magazine, *October, November 1987.*

"Religions need to reassess homosexuality in a positive context with their belief systems. . .Religions should also take responsibility for providing their families and membership with positive information about homosexuality that discourages the oppression of lesbians and gay men."

— *Paul Gibson, San Francisco social worker and gay activist, "Gay Male and Lesbian Youth Suicide", paper in HHS Task Force on Youth Suicide, January 1989, p. 3-135.*

Gay Strategy: Desensitize Americans

"The first order of business is desensitization of the American public concerning gays and gay rights. To desensitize the public is to help it view homosexuality with indifference instead of with keen emotion…You can forget about trying to persuade the masses that homosexuality is a good thing. But if you can get them to think that it is just another thing with a shrug of their shoulders, then your battle for legal and social rights is virtually won.

— *Marshall Kirk and Erastes Pill, "The Overhauling of Straight America,"* Guide Magazine, *October, November 1987.*

26   THE GAY RIGHTS MOVEMENT

CIVIL RIGHTS UNDER ATTACK

Sue Anderson

Sue Anderson wrote the following for The Nonviolent Activist, *which is published six times a year by the* War Resisters League. *The League affirms that all war is a crime against humanity.*

Points to Consider:

1. Summarize the impact of Amendment 2.

2. How was the "special rights" message effectively used by the far right?

3. Define what Anderson means by the "stealth strategy" of the right.

4. How does Anderson propose that gay rights activists counter the radical right agenda?

Sue Anderson, "Lesbian and Gay Civil Rights Under Attack," **The Nonviolent Activist**, a publication of the War Resisters League, May-June, 1993.

I do not believe that the 1964 Civil Rights Act would have passed had it been put to a vote of the people.

The passage in November 1992 of Colorado's Amendment 2 set off shock waves around the country among those concerned with civil rights. People are talking about similarities to laws passed early in Hitler's regime, the rise of the religious right, and the need — now more than ever — to join together and analyze all oppressions and their linkages. Those of us in Colorado are at the center of such discussions, and in this article I will look at some of the lessons learned by the Colorado experience and the ramifications of the Colorado boycott.

First, to clarify Amendment 2's impact, it overturns existing civil rights protections based on sexual orientation in Denver, Boulder and Aspen as well as Governor Romer's Executive Order giving protections for gays, lesbians and bisexuals. It also makes it unconstitutional for municipalities and government entities to give such protections in the future. A suit has been filed challenging the constitutionality of the law and a temporary injunction was granted in January with a trial date set in October. The law is on hold for the moment, but this is a case which may go to the Supreme Court and take several years to resolve.

COLORADANS FOR FAMILY VALUES

The ramifications of the successful campaign by the far right in Colorado, under the name of Coloradans for Family Values (CFV), are far-reaching. CFV equated protected status for gays, lesbians and bisexuals with "special rights", a strategy produced at the Heritage Foundation. Do persons in protected classes based on ethnicity, race, marital status or religion also have "special rights"? Discussions about the vote in Colorado and elsewhere often ignore the core issue of basic civil rights protections, because many people continue to believe that this was about "special rights" and "no protected status" for any group. The "special rights" message was a simple one — and obviously an effective tactic.

The reality is that lesbian, gay and bisexual people are not protected from discrimination in any way federally, in Colorado, or in most states. Too many voters want to believe that the agenda of the far right is benign and really has something to do with "family values". However, their agenda is based on a "stealth" strategy of passing restrictive laws and electing narrowly focused candidates at

all levels of government.

The stealth strategy of the right is dangerous and well planned. That the ballot initiatives in Colorado and Oregon were markedly different from each other in language appears to have been well planned. National attention focused on the vehement, noxious language in Oregon (placed on the ballot by the Oregon Citizens Alliance) while the seemingly benign ballot initiative of the Coloradans for Family Values slipped by. Despite differences these ballot initiatives have the same effects of denying civil rights protections to a particular class of people. Work is already underway in at least ten or twelve other states to pass Colorado-style initiatives. I do not believe that the 1964 Civil Rights Act would have passed had it been put to a vote of the people. Should the rights of any minority be decided by the majority?...

A CALL FOR UNITY

Lesbians and gays are not the first targets of the religious right, nor will we be the last. Their stealth campaigns are striking all levels of government from school boards and neighborhood organizations on up the political ladder. Ballot initiatives are popping up all over the

GAY RIGHTS

A Colorado court today wrestles with the question of whether homosexuals fit the legal definition of a minority. The answer will determine whether a state judge was correct in preventing Amendment 2 — an anti-gay-rights measure — from becoming law...

Last year, Colorado voters narrowly approved the statewide initiative, which prohibits local governments from enacting laws that protect gay rights. Two months after the vote, Denver District Judge Jeffrey Bayless barred the amendment from becoming law. He believes the law is very likely unconstitutional. While today's hearing is an appeal of Bayless' ruling, many see it as a first step to a ruling by the U.S. Supreme Court.

Debbie Howlett, "Issue of Gay Rights," **USA Today**, October 12, 1993

country organized by groups with names such as the Idaho Citizens Alliance, or Minnesotans for Family Values. All of these groups have some connections to national groups such as the American Family Association, the Christian Coalition, the National Legal Foundation or Focus on the Family. They have developed effective messages which seem benign until interpreted in a larger context. Their influence over our daily lives is growing on a subtle level, and their infiltration of leadership positions is preparation for larger battles.

The progressive movement has not always been supportive of lesbian, gay and bisexual issues nor have lesbians, gays and bisexuals necessarily been supportive of other issues. Those of us who have worked across issue lines seem to be the exception, not the norm. This must change on both sides if we are to defeat the radical right agenda. The development of stronger community-based organizing is critical. The insidious presence of the radical right is not going to be defeated without talking face-to-face with our neighbors and working together across issue lines.

27   THE GAY RIGHTS MOVEMENT

UPHOLDING FAMILY VALUES

Don Feder

Don Feder is a prominent conservative journalist, spokesperson and frequent contributor to The Conservative Chronicle, *a weekly publication based in Des Moines, Iowa.*

Points to Consider:

1. Compare Colorado's Question 2 with Oregon's Question 9.

2. What was the intention of Question 9?

3. What evidence does Feder present to justify denying "persecuted minority" status to gays?

4. What sort of activity does Oregon's alliance cite as a "deadly assault" on our moral code?

Don Feder, "Ballot Measures Spell Trouble for Gay Rights," **Conservative Chronicle**, 1992. By permission of Don Feder and Creators Syndicate.

If gays are a persecuted minority, where is the evidence of their suffering?

A flyer distributed by the New York Democratic State Committee during the past campaign showed just how far the Clinton camp was willing to go in pandering to homosexuals. The appeal — which looked like an ad for a telephone sex service — featured a composite photo, with the heads of Clinton and Gore on the bodies of two bare-chested, muscular, young men posed in Bermuda shorts and cut-off jeans.

On the reverse was a list of postdated IOUs, including repeal of the ban on homosexuals in the military and passage of a federal gay rights law. Before the next administration presses forward with this dubious agenda, it might consider the fate of pro-family initiatives on statewide ballots in Colorado and Oregon this year for an idea of the opposition that awaits such a move.

QUESTION 2

Colorado's Question 2 prohibits the state and its political subdivisions from enacting gay rights laws. Oregon's Question 9 went further, requiring state agencies, including schools, "to assist in setting a standard" that recognizes homosexuality as deviant behavior to be avoided. In a post-election analysis, the pollster for KATU-TV in Portland declared that without this mandate the initiative would have passed.

As it was, Oregon lost, 44 percent to 56 percent, while Colorado carried, 53 percent to 47 percent. One was a triumphant advance, the other a moral victory. Both states are well outside the Bible Belt, intellectually as well as geographically. Clinton carried each by comfortable margins. Colorado has been represented in the U.S. Senate by the likes of Gary Hart and Tim Wirth. Oregon boasts the two most liberal Republicans in the Senate, Mark Hatfield and Robert Packwood.

Proponents were Davids confronting Goliaths of the cultural elite. The entire political establishment of Colorado lined up against Question 2, including the governor, the mayor of Denver, the wife of the Republican Speaker of the House, the League of Women Voters and the United Methodist Church. Major contributors to the campaign against the question included the Colorado Education Association, Digital Equipment, Apple Computer and Bell West.

FUNDING GAP

Colorado for Family Values, the measure's sponsor, was outspent by better than 2-to-1 ($300,000 to $700,000). Television stations in Denver, which has 75 percent of the state's voters, refused to air their ads. One that included footage from a gay rights parade was deemed too provocative. It's quite all right for militants to carry on as they do at these galas, but it's extreme provocation to discuss the same.

In Oregon the funding gap was even more pronounced — $400,000 for the Oregon's Citizen's Alliance, which backed the question, to $1.5 million for the opposition. Even such ordinarily nonpolitical groups as the American Library Association, Oregon Medical Association and Portland YMCA lined up against the measure.

The debate revolved around rights vs values. Opponents argued the initiatives would deny civil liberties protections to homosexuals. Proponents countered that passage wouldn't change anyone's status as a citizen. The aim was to prevent the social sanction of homosexual conduct, to stop state subsidies for homosexuality and to get activists out of our faces.

If gays are a persecuted minority, where is the evidence of their suffering? Literature for CVF noted that homosexuals have an average household income of $55,430 compared to a national average of $32,286. The usual indices of discrimination — substandard housing and employment, poverty — are absent.

SEXUAL MINORITY

Opponents tried to portray the measures as aggressive, an attempt to ghettoize a "sexual minority". Supporters viewed themselves as the guardians of a moral code under deadly assault.

Portland's gay rights parade gets public funding. The city's police chief trumpets an effort to recruit homosexuals for the force. The South Eugene High School has an annual Gay Awareness Week, where homosexuals are invited to distribute material to students and proselytize for their lifestyle. Last year, Queer Nation, the movement's goon squad, was allowed to set up a literature table at the school. This, said the moral meanies of Citizens Alliance, is what we're trying to stop.

That the Alliance managed to attract 43 percent of the vote, notwithstanding everything that was thrown against it, demonstrates the degree of public unease on the subject. That the Colorado initiative passed is nothing short of miraculous. If the president-elect wants to experience the type of savage combat he missed in Vietnam, he could get it here. In at least two states, pro-family forces are ready to field seasoned veterans.

WHAT IS SEX BIAS?

This activity may be used as an individualized study guide for students in libraries and resource centers or as a discussion catalyst in small group and classroom discussions.

Many readers are unaware that written material usually expresses an opinion or bias. The skill to read with insight and understanding requires the ability to detect different kinds of bias. **Political bias, race bias, sex bias, ethnocentric bias** and **religious bias** are five basic kinds of opinions expressed in editorials and literature that attempt to persuade. This activity will focus on sex bias defined in the glossary below.

FIVE KINDS OF EDITORIAL OPINION OR BIAS

Sex Bias — the expression of dislike for and/or feeling of superiority over a person because of gender or sexual preference

Race Bias — the expression of dislike for and/or feeling of superiority over a racial group

Ethnocentric Bias — the expression of a belief that one's own group, race, religion, culture or nation is superior. Ethnocentric persons judge others by their own standards and values.

Political Bias — the expression of opinions and attitudes about government-related issues on the local, state, national or international level

Religious Bias — the expression of a religious belief or attitude

---

Guidelines

Read through the following statements and decide which ones represent **sex bias**. Evaluate each statement by using the method indicated below.

- Mark (F) for any factual statements.

- Mark (S) for statements that reflect any sex bias.

- Mark (O) for statements of opinion that reflect other kinds of opinion or bias.

- Mark (N) for any statements that you are not sure about.

_____1. Allow gay marriages and openly gay people in the military as fruits of living in a civil, public society. But don't legislate private tolerance.

_____2. There seem to be very few happy heterosexuals.

_____3. Every opinion survey shows that people who say they have a gay friend or family member are two or three times as likely to support gay rights than are those who say they know no gay people.

_____4. Something is abnormally wrong with prevailing society when it causes parents to reject sons and daughters due to a condition that is largely, if not entirely, involuntary.

_____5. Homosexuals are more promiscuous than heterosexuals.

_____6. Not for thirty years has a class of Americans endured the peculiar pain and exhilaration of having their civil rights and moral worth — their very humanness — debated at every level of public life.

_____7. Homosexuals seek validation for their way of life — through the manipulation of law and culture.

_____8. Many in the gay political movement wrongly believe that it is their mission to gain private tolerance of homosexuality.

_____9. Homosexuals do not need special protection.

_____10. A great majority of child molesters are heterosexuals.

_____11. If gays are a persecuted minority, where is the evidence of their suffering?

_____12. Granting special protection to homosexuals would also take rights away from others.

_____13. Homosexuality is usually a brief phase which people can grow out of.

_____14. Rather than being considered a minority group, homosexuals are more accurately described as a special interest group.

_____15. Homosexuals have a history of failure in their personal and sexual relationships.

_____16. The 1964 Civil Rights Act would not have been passed if it had been put to a vote of the people.

_____17. Homosexuality sometimes stems from a neurotic fear of people of the opposite sex.

_____18. Using civil rights arguments to promote homosexuality is an exploitation of good people's sympathy.

Additional Activities

1. Locate three examples of **sex bias** in the readings from Chapter Five.

2. Make up five one-sentence statements that would all be examples of **sex bias.**

BIBLIOGRAPHY

"After the March Is Over: A Flurry of Incidents Shows That Gay Rights Have a Way to Go." **Time** 10 May 1993: 25-6.

Allis, T. "Saying It Loud." **People Weekly** 10 May 1993: 49-50.

Ames, K. "Domesticated Bliss: New Laws Are Making It Official for Gay or Live-in Straight Couples. **Newsweek** 23 Mar. 1992: 62-3.

Atchison, S.D. "Bashing Gays — and Business." **Business Week** 7 Dec. 1992: 42.

Atchison, S.D. "Herbal Teas in Hot Water." **Business Week** 1 Mar. 1993: 42+.

Baumann, P.D. "Sodom & Begorra." **Commonweal** 9 Apr. 1993: 5-6.

Beck, M. "The Impact on Gay Political Power." **Newsweek** 26 Apr. 1993: 57.

Bethell, T. "Trojan Army." **The American Spectator** Apr. 1992: 20-1.

Blotcher, J. "Gay Body Bias." **Utne Reader** May/June 1992: 56-7.

Bower, B. "Gene Influence Tied to Sexual Orientation." **Science News** 4 Jan. 1992: 16.

Bowman, J. "Lavender & Purple." **Commonweal** 24 Apr. 1992: 5-6.

"Can Gays and Lesbians Come Out to Be Faithful Catholics." **U.S. Catholic** Aug. 1992: 6-13.

Carlin, D.R. Jr. "Abortion, Gay Rights and the Social Contract." **America** 27 Feb. 1993: 6-10.

"Church Leaders on Gay Issue." **The Christian Century** 3 Mar. 1993: 233.

Clift, E. "How the Candidates Play to Gays." **Newsweek** 14 Sept. 1992: 40.

Corliss, R. "Colorado's Deep Freeze." **Time** 14 Dec. 1992: 54-5.

"Courting Injustice." **National Review** 1 Mar. 1993: 16+.

Cowan, M. "Out on the Screen." **Utne Reader** May/June 1992: 30+.

Crain, C. "Gay Glue." **The New Republic** 10 May 1993: 16.

Dahir, M.S. "Coming Out at the Barrel." **The Progressive** June 1992: 14.

Dallas, J. "Born Gay?" **Christianity Today** 22 June 1992: 20-3.

DeCosse, D.E. "The Catholic Case for Inclusion." **America** 8 May 1993: 15-6.

"Don't Lie to Homosexuals." **Christianity Today** 17 Mar. 1993: 17.

Duignan-Cabrera, A. "Gay GOPs: The Enemy Within." **Newsweek** 24 Aug. 1992: 43.

Eastland, T. "Newsweek Acts Up." **The American Spectator** Nov. 1992: 58-9.

Ehrenriech, B. "The Gap Between Gay and Straight." **Time** 10 May 1993: 76.

Ellis, A. "Are Gays and Lesbians Emotionally Disturbed?" **The Humanist** Sept./Oct. 1992: 33-5.

Ellis, A. "What Are Sexual Perversions?" **The Humanist** May/June 1992: 35.

Estes, C.P. "Singing Over the Bones: The Colorado Boycott." **Publishers Weekly** 14 Dec. 1992: 64.

Fineman, H. "Marching to the Mainstream." **Newsweek** 3 May 1993: 42-5.

"For Gays, Wedding Bells May Soon Ring." **Newsweek** 17 May 1993: 62.

Friend, R.A. "Undoing Homophobia in Schools." **The Education Digest** Feb. 1993: 62-6.

Fumento, M. "How Many Gays?" **National Review** 26 Apr. 1993: 28-9.

Gates, H.L. "Blacklash?" **The New Yorker** 17 May 1993: 42-4.

"Gay Man Licensed in SBC." **The Christian Century** 29 Apr. 1992: 448-9.

"The Gay Vice Squad." **National Review** 19 Oct. 1992: 19.

"Gays Under Fire." **Newsweek** 14 Sept. 1992: 34-41.

George, T. "Baptists and Gay Marriage." **Christianity Today** 18 May 1992: 15.

Goldberg, S. "What Is Normal?" **National Review** 3 Feb. 1992: 36-9.

"Hanky Panky: Deciphering the Gay Bandana Code." **Utne Reader** Jan./Feb. 1993: 137.

Hazlett, T.W. "Queer Tactics." **Reason** Mar. 1993: 66.

Henry, W.A. "The Gay White Way." **Time** 17 May 1993: 62-3.

Henry, W.A. "An Identity Forged in Flames." **Time** 3 Aug. 1992: 35-7.

Henry, W.A. "Not Marching Together." **Time** 3 May 1993: 50-1.

Hitchens, C. "Minority Report." **The Nation** 10 May 1993: 618.

Holden, C. "Twin Study Links Genes to Homosexuality." **Science** 3 Jan. 1992: 33.

"Homosexuality and Cognition." **Science** 31 Jan. 1992: 539.

Horowitz, D. "The Queer Fellows." **The American Spectator** Jan. 1993: 42-6+.

Hoyt, R.G. "Is It Ideology?" **Commonweal** 21 May 1993: 4-5.

Hume, S. "Bum Steer." **The American Spectator** Dec. 1992: 47.

Kaufman, L.A. "Queer Guerrillas in Tinseltown." **The Progressive** July 1992: 36-7.

Killacky, J.R. "Angels and the NEA." **Utne Reader** Nov./Dec. 1992: 134-5.

Koestenbaum, W. "Confessions of an Opera Queen." **Harper's** Feb. 1993: 35-6+.

Kopkind, A. "The Gay Moment." **The Nation** 3 May 1993: 577+.

Kopkind, A. "Paint It Pink." **The Nation** 17 May 1993: 652-3.

"Lame-duck Group Issues Homosexuality Report." **The Christian Century** 11 Nov. 1992: 1024-5.

"The Last Prejudice." **The Progressive** Oct. 1992: 9-10.

Lewis, M. "Straight Answer." **The New Republic** 10 May 1993: 22.

"Live & Let Live." **Commonweal** 15 Jan. 1993: 3-4.

"Malice Toward Some." **The New Yorker** 26 Oct. 1992: 4+.

Markowitz, L.M. "Do Gays and Lesbians Get Along?" **Utne Reader** Jan./Feb. 1993: 58-9.

Markowitz, L.M. "Money, Honey: Lesbian and Gay Couples Face Special Economic Challenges." **Utne Reader** Sept./Oct. 1992: 62.

Marshall, E. "Sex on the Brain." **Science** 31 July 1992: 620-1.

Mathews, J. "From Closet to Mainstream." **Newsweek** 1 June 1992: 62.

Meyer, M.R. and K.L. Woodward. "Onward Muscular Christians." **Newsweek** 1 Mar. 1993: 68.

Minkowitz, D. "Outlawing Gays." **The Nation** 19 Oct. 1992: 420-1.

Nagourney, A. "Homophiliac: Clinton and Gays." **The New Republic** 4-11 Jan. 1993: 16-17.

Osborne, R. "Sex as Crime." **The Progressive** May 1992: 15.

"The Other Minority." **The New Republic** 30 Mar. 1992: 7.

Painton, P. "After Willie Horton: Are Gays Next?" **Time** 3 Aug. 1992: 42.

Painton, P. "The Shrinking Ten Percent." **Time** 26 Apr. 1993: 27-9.

"Partners for Life." **Time** 22 Feb. 1993: 43.

Pattullo, E.L. "Gay Rights." **Commentary** Mar. 1993: 2+.

Pattullo, E.L. "Straight Talk About Gays." **Commentary** Dec. 1992: 21-4.

"Pope Backs Hate Crimes." **The Nation** 24 Aug. 1992: 157.

Rabey, S. "Amendment 2 Sharpens Clash Over Gay Rights." **Christianity Today** 11 Jan. 1993: 57.

Rabey, S. "Focus Under Fire." **Christianity Today** 8 Mar. 1993: 48+.

"Schlafly's Son: Out of the GOP Closet." **Newsweek** 28 Sept. 1992: 18.

Schmalz, J. "Gay Politics Goes Mainstream." **The New York Times Magazine** 11 Oct. 1992: 18-21+.

Tierney, W.G. "Building Academic Communities of Difference: Gays, Lesbians, and Bisexuals on Campus." **Change** Mar./Apr. 1992: 40-6.

Tobias, A.P. "Three-dollar Bills." **Time** 23 Mar. 1992: 47.

Townsend, J. "The Private Life of a Teacher." **The Progressive** May 1992: 37.

Traver, N. "Why Foley Stood Idle." **Time** 13 Apr. 1992: 29.

Tucker, S. "Lesbian Witches, Socialist Sodomites, and Cultural War." **The Humanist** Jan./Feb. 1993: 42-3.

Tuller, D. "Political Asylum for Gays?" **The Nation** 19 Apr. 1993: 520.

Turque, B. "Press 'I' for the Christian Right." **Newsweek** 8 Feb. 1993: 28.

Tuohey, J. F. "The C.D.F. and Homosexuals: Rewriting the Moral Tradition." **America** 12 Sept. 1992: 136-8.

"UMC Bishop Rejects Gay Union Liturgies." **The Christian Century** 21 Oct. 1992: 928-30.

"UMC on Homosexuality." **The Christian Century** 20-27 May 1992: 536-7.

Uribe, V. "Project 10 Addresses Needs of Gay and Lesbian Youth." **The Education Digest** Oct. 1992: 50-4.

Vaid, U. "After Identity." **The New Republic** 10 May 1993: 28.

Vidal, G. "Abuzz and Atwitter." **The Nation** 27 Jan. 1992: 74.

Wakelee-Lynch, J. "Should I Stay or Should I Go?" **Utne Reader** Jan./Feb. 1992: 40+.

Wilson, B.L. "On Oregon's Ballot, a Measure Aimed at Gays." **Governing** Oct. 1992: 18-19.

Zeman, N. and M.R. Meyer. "No Special Rights for Gays: Colorado Voters Pass an Anti-gay Amendment, with Disturbing Results." **Newsweek** 23 Nov. 1992: 32.